C000144669

LLŶN CYCLE GUIDE

LLŶN CYCLE GUIDE

Phil Horsley

First published in 2012

© Phil Horsley

© Llygad Gwalch 2012

ISBN: 978-1-84524-185-8

Cover design: Lynwen Jones

Published by Llygad Gwalch,
Ysgubor Plas, Llwyndyrys,
Pwllheli, Gwynedd, Wales, LL53 6NG,

www.carreg-gwalch.com

Dedicated to Annie

Llŷn Area of Outstanding Natural Beauty (AONB)

Llŷn is one of only 5 AONB's in Wales, and has been designated in order to sustain and safeguard the area's natural beauty which includes the landscape, wildlife, historical features and the unique social character. You can find more information and the latest updates on the AONB website: www.ahne-llyn-aonb.org

Llŷn Peninsula

1 Lôn Eifion
2 Clynnog
3 Around Yr Eifl
4 The mountains of Nefyn
5 Nefyn - Tudweiliog
6 Garn Fadryn
7 North Coast Explorer
8 The End
9 Aberdaron Loop
10 Rhiw - Phew

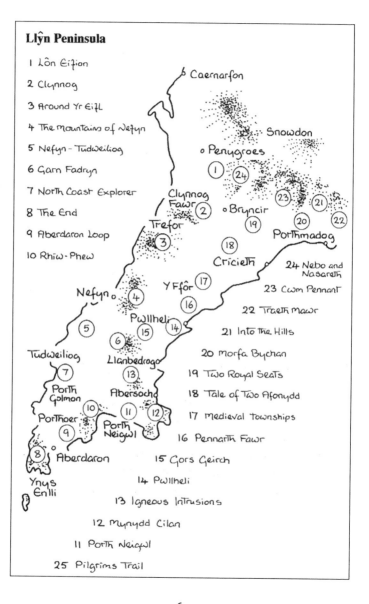

24 Nebo and Nasareth
23 Cwm Pennant
22 Traeth Mawr
21 Into the Hills
20 Morfa Bychan
19 Two Royal Seats
18 Tale of Two Afonydd
17 Medieval Townships
16 Pennarth Fawr
15 Gors Geirch
14 Pwllheli
13 Igneous Intrusions
12 Mynydd Cilan
11 Porth Neigwl
25 Pilgrims Trail

Contents

Introduction

This is a guide book to cycling on the Llŷn Peninsula.

The Llŷn Peninsula

This guide book is designed primarily for the English-speaking visitor, but the place-names are, of course, Welsh, and so, throughout this book the Welsh names are used, accompanied by the English name where appropriate. So it's a guide to cycling in Llŷn.

Strictly Llŷn is the end bit, Pwllheli and beyond, but that makes no cycling sense, so I've included the whole peninsula, bounded to the east by the mountains, and the sea on both sides. I've stopped at the narrowest points, going North that's Afon Llyfni (*afon* = river), and the villages of Pontllyfni and Llanllyfni, and going south and east the guide stops at Porthmadog.

The Cyclist

Cyclists come in all shapes and sizes. I've ridden on a cycle path with a pack of day-glo'd youngsters barely out of stabilisers, dashing hither and thither like whirligig beetles on a pond. I've watched professionals climbing prodigious hills faster than I can move on the flat, and chatting. My home town was full of black roadsters with rod brakes and no gears, one child on the crossbar, another in the fold-down seat behind the rider's bottom, and shopping dangling from the handlebars in string bags.

In theory, I've divided the rides in this book into one of three categories:-

- **Family Rides**, up to 10km, preferably with a 'destination' as my partner calls it, i.e. somewhere to find at least an ice-cream.

- **Popular Rides**, basically everything from 10km to 50km, which I'll qualify with a grading.
- **Enthusiasts Rides**, over 50km. Although I'm basically assuming that enthusiasts will simply stick a couple of the popular rides together, and the book is laid out to make this easy.

A Note about Route finding.

You'll get lost. It's really easy. Lots of small back roads twisting around like a dog chasing it's tail, and a limited number of finger posts. The route finding maps in this book are diagrammatic, based on the normal cycling practise of counting junctions, first right, left and left again etc, which saves constant map inspections. It is a good idea to carry a map though, and the 1:50,000 maps of Llŷn Peninsula (number 123) and Porthmadog and Dolgellau (number 124) cover more or less the whole patch.

The Naming of Parts.

The more discerning of you will have noticed discrepancies between the naming of some places in this book, their names on O.S. maps and road signs on the ground. This is a hot potato.

Let's start with the easy one. some places have English and Welsh names, e.g. Porth Neigwl (*Hell's Mouth*), Porthoer (*Whistling Sands*), with the names being entirely unrelated. Though you may still see '*Whistling Sands*' and '*Hells Mouth*' on road signs, they are being phased out in favour of the Welsh name. Sometimes both names will be included. It used to be common to see the English name scored out with red paint. You could say that the English names are considered almost as nicknames these days.

The notion of a standard spelling of a place name is a relatively modern one, with 'official' versions being used in such places as O.S. maps, postal addresses and on road signs. In Llŷn the definitive 'official' version has been clouded by both Anglicisation and the Welsh language itself. Not so long ago it was Government policy to Anglicise the 'Llŷn Peninsula'. Some road signs still exist from that era, for example there is at least one road sign which directs you to '*Nevin*'. Others can catch you out. Apart from the individual Welsh consonants which contain two letters, i.e. 'll' and 'dd', only the letter 'n' is doubled in Welsh, which means that 'Cricieth' is the correct version, and '*Criccieth*' is Anglicised.

Now we come to the bits which still confuse me. One is mutation. In Welsh, in some circumstances some consonants mutate. Is it too far fetched to bring in Star Trek here? Although the weird crinkly creatures look different on the surface, it is obvious that they are humans with a makeover. Some even talk in a recognisable language. So it is with mutations, and the common ones are p to b, t to d, c to g, b to f and m to f, (examples Hen+plas= Henblas; Llan+St Tudwen= Llandudwen; Llan+St Cian=Llangian; Ffynnon+Mair (Mary)= Ffynnon Fair; Ffynnon+Byw (alive) = Ffynnon Fyw).

The other source of confusion for me is the separation of a name into two words, or the use of a hyphen. For example Porthgolman is written on O.S. maps as Porth Golman. But then I've never got a grip on the differences between the English Brough, Burgh and Borough either. Unfortunately O.S. maps do not always follow the correct spellings of place-names.

The Cycling

My daughter Rosie, when she was six, never liked to cycle uphill. Route finding on Llŷn was a real challenge. The cycling here is fabulous, as good as anywhere in the country and better than most, but there are quite a few short hills. The Reverend Bingley, from Cambridge, travelling on foot in 1798, advised visitors against penetrating Llŷn, by suggesting it 'may not be interesting to many tourists; and very few would think their trouble repaid in visiting the extreme parts of the promontory.' I am suggesting that the Rev. Bingley was 'nesh' (as we say in Yorkshire), and that you should embrace the rising road as your friend, as indeed Rosie does now, and you will be rewarded with some joyous wheeling.

Some cyclists, often lycra clad and with keen noses, prefer the A and B-roads for the sheer thrill of a well tuned body and machine operating in perfect harmony. I've been there in my younger days. Mainly, in this guide, I'm going to tempt you onto those quiet back roads where, even at the height of summer, the hum of a motor is a cause for comment. On the road on which I live, on a normal day, I can count 4 or 5 cars, a flock of sheep, Mr Llewellyn in his mini-pickup with the 4-headed hydra of a dog in the back, and the postman (hi, Eryl). The Authorities are looking towards the designation of some of these lanes as 'Quiet Roads/Rural Lanes' to control their use and the speed of traffic, and give priority to pedestrians, cyclists and horses. It is my suggestion that we do it ourselves, and the more cyclists the better.

What makes Llŷn special?
Firstly, the landscape is designated as 'special'. The coastline has a degree of special protection, as does the inshore sea itself. Half the land is designated as an Area of Outstanding Natural Beauty (AONB). In the overall master plan for Llŷn it is recommended that wind turbines be refused entirely in the AONB, and elsewhere approved only if they are 'small scale/ community or domestic'.

Some of the patterns in the landscape that you see are medieval, and the settlement pattern can be traced back to the Dark Ages, but much of the countryside is 200 years old, dating back to the Enclosures, when many of the tracks were improved and new straight lanes were made, with a clawdd on either side, an earth bank topped with a thorn hedge. Towards the mountains the lanes are lined with stone walls, the older ones twisting and turning as if they were dancing up the hillsides.

Llŷn is an unhurried, friendly place with a distinct 'different culture' for an English person. It is the stated aim of the planners to protect the 'social, linguistic and cultural fabric of the communities.'

This western peninsula has retained its historical character and heritage, though the twentieth century has brought with it the silent erosion of local work, with farming in Llŷn hanging on a precarious thread, but culturally it is a wonderful place in which to live, and to visit, and well worth protecting and respecting.

For me a part of cycling is to explore the interaction of people and place. I've cycled all over Britain and even in the most ugly, dirty places there are stories to be heard and changes to witness. It may seem timeless here on Llŷn, and one generation of a family tends to follow the last in coming here on holiday, but it is changing all the time and my aim in this book is to enable the cyclist not only to read the landscape, but to picture life as it is, and has been lived here.

The seaside holiday season here is short, really only June to August, though there are visitors around from Easter to late October, and this is built into the rhythm of life here. Outside the towns, the countryside is governed by the farming year. Lambing is early, from December onwards, and then there follows the usual cycle of silaging, shearing, haymaking, hedge trimming, corn harvesting and muck spreading. Much of the farming is as organic as can be without the label, with little fertiliser used apart from dung, and hardly any chemical spraying.

Llŷn has significant problems which are not immediately apparent. It has a low wage economy, dependent on seasonal tourist work and agriculture (farming incomes have fallen significantly in recent years), and high levels of poverty. It also has an aging population as young people leave the area for jobs or training. The demand for holiday and second homes has raised the level of house prices beyond the reach of many local people.

Hazards for the Cyclist

The A Roads
Personally, given a choice, I will avoid using the A487 Llanwnda (near Caernarfon) to Porthmadog road. The A499 Llanwnda to Pwllheli road has a cycle track from Aberdesach to Llanaelhaearn, and there are plans to extend this to Glynllifon to link up with minor roads to Caernarfon. Until this happens the 3 km stretch from Aberdesach to Pontllyfni is not at all pleasant. Again, I'll avoid cycling the A499 from Llanaelhaearn to Pwllheli.

The A497 Nefyn to Pwllheli road is OK, but most traffic is travelling 60 mph on this narrowish road.

The A499/A497 road along the southern coast of Llŷn is a curate's egg. Again there are plans for a cycle-friendly route right along the southern coast from Abersoch to Porthmadog, but who knows when this will happen given today's financial constraints. As it is, you end up on the A499/A497. The Abersoch-Llanbedrog bit is not too bad; Llanbedrog-Pwllheli is awful, narrow, fast, dangerous; Pwllheli-Abererch is OK and as I write a cycle path is under construction, then there's a cycle path almost to Llanystumdwy, and the bit to Criccieth is not too bad (some cyclists use the footpaths – naughty people); Criccieth-Porthmadog I don't like. It's not particularly fast but it's narrowish, busy and bustling, with a hilly section.

The B Roads and minor roads
The B 4354 was built as a turnpike road, from Tan-y-graig (south of Nefyn) to Chwilog/Llanystumdwy on the A497. It is not dangerous or particularly busy, but it is used nowadays much as

it was intended, as a fast route into Llŷn, and traffic fairly tanks along. It is useful for getting from A to B, but not with any great pleasure, and for nervous or young or unconfident cyclists it may not be the best route to take.

The two B Roads to Aberdaron, from Llanbedrog and from Llanealhaearn (through Nefyn) take most of the traffic in this part of the world, but that's not saying much, and only the boy-racers are dangerous. There is one long-distance cycle path, Lôn Eifion, from Caernarfon to Bryncir.

On the back roads meeting cars is a matter of negotiation. Most drivers are courteous and friendly, and waving is the norm. Livestock moves along these back roads. Sheep are usually fairly indifferent; cows are interested but suspicious; I met three running bulls once, that was memorable; and then there are horses. I don't know why, but bikes make horses twitch. "Scary cyclists" we've been called (by the rider not the horse). Talk to them (the riders not the horses) well before you catch them up. You'll notice the ears twitch (the horses not the riders). In the horses head this doesn't come across as nice person on a harmless vehicle, but, danger, jump ship, revert to bolt-across-the-plains mode. A good rider will notice the twitch. If they don't, take extra care, it's a long way down (I've seen them fall). Despite being an authorised road vehicle, you can whistle, and talk, and sing and say "Dring-Dring".

Dogs. On Llŷn there are lots of dogs. Most have a Hey Dude sort of attitude but some enjoy barking and chasing, and basically scaring the living daylights out of cyclists. I've never been bitten on Llŷn, and I am coming round to the idea of gently conversing with the snarling dog about the State of the World, though I do realise that there is an inconsistency here in that most dogs will only understand Welsh.

The Cycling Code

I hate those cycling codes which consist of a dozen 'don'ts'. Don't speed, smile, hop, skip, jump, don't twist again like we did last summer. So here's a different Cycling Code.

1. The bicycle is the most flexible, useful, green, enjoyable, inexpensive, healthy, quiet, invigorating mode of transport ever invented. All hail to thee Kirkpatrick MacMillan. Enjoy it.

Tip: if you are unfit, the more you ride the fitter you'll become, but you may struggle on the hills initially. Two things happen, the muscles in your legs begin to ache, and you get out of breath. These are related. Basically, as I understand it, your heart and lungs work together to deliver oxygen to your muscles via the blood cells. There the oxygen combines with the fuel from your food to produce energy. You will achieve the delivery of more oxygen by breathing at a controlled rate rather than panting or gasping. Concentrate on steady, controlled out breaths and the in breath looks after itself. If your muscles really ache or cramp, ease down, drop down a gear, and stretch your muscles when you get a chance. It is very unlikely to be lactic acid, which you control by warming up and warming down.

The other most common problem for cyclists is in the knees. Make sure your saddle is correctly adjusted, and your feet sit correctly on your pedals so your knees aren't twisted in any way. The most important thing is not to push it, keep your cadence high (that's the rhythm of your legs turning) and use your gears to keep the same cadence all day.

OK, there is another common problem. Trouble in the delicate posterior area. They recommend that you break in your saddle. In practise this means breaking in your bum to fit the saddle. If soreness occurs, emollient creams, like Sudocream, works better than Vaseline. My partner swears by sheep's wool (it's the lanolin), and I have heard (but not tried) that riders in the Tour used to use a banana. Prevention is better than cure, and the double-gusset stands tall in the list of Top Ten Inventions of All Time.

2. You are proper. You are not some low-life gutter-loving pariah that threatens the stability of the Nation-State. The Highway Code says that you should ride single file on narrow country roads. Hang on, how come it's all right for two people in a Range Rover to sit side by side, and you can't? I agree it often makes sense to get out of the way of a ton of hurtling metal, but you need to learn to ride in the road, not in the gutter. Make vehicles overtake you, not try to squeeze by.

3. There should be a fellowship of cyclists. We're different, I could even say superior. Meet and greet. I have seen the future – three riders in their eighties, fit and strong and enjoying every minute of swooping along together. I want to be there when the time comes.

4. In the Highway Code there are lots of 'shoulds' for cyclists, and these are mostly common sense. Basically, there are three laws. At night the bike must have front and rear lights and a reflector. Flashing lights are permitted. You must not ride on a pavement. And you must not ride a) in a dangerous, careless or inconsiderate manner, and b) ride when under the influence of drink or drugs. The fines are as follows:-
     – Dangerous cycling £2,500
     – Careless cycling £1,000
     – Cycling on a pavement £500

5. On a bicycle, exposed to, and communicating with the wind, the sun, the people, the past, all creatures great and small, you are the future and you are ideally placed to tap into the cosmic consciousness. I've seen a bicycle made entirely out of wood; I've seen a convertible cycle beginning it's crossing of Morecambe Bay; I've seen a pigeon with a broken wing riding on the handlebars of a cyclist circumnavigating the British Isles; I've seen

a unicyclist juggling and bouncing on a trampoline (I winced every time he bounced). I have only one recommendation. Pump up your tyres hard. I've seen a couple on a tandem after they had a blow out riding downhill. It wasn't a pretty sight.

Cycle Shops and Repair

Llŷn Cycle Centre
Lower Ala Road
Pwllheli
tel. 01758 612414

K K Cycles
141 High Street
Porthmadog
tel. 01766 512310

Cycle Hire

Llŷn Cycle Hire
Aberdaron
tel. 01758 760532
info@llyncyclehire.co.uk

Cycling Organisations

Clwb Beicio Llŷn Cycling Club
www.beicio-llyn-cycling.com
They organise runs, racing, MTB, time trialling, cyclo-cross, including popular sessions around the track at Glasfryn.

Gwynedd Cycling Association
contact through Clwb Beicio Llŷn.

CTC North Wales
www.cyclingnorthwales.co.uk
www.cyclebreakswales is the official website of Cycling Wales, a part of the tourist organisation VisitWales.

The Weather

According to the Met Office the summer averages in Llŷn show the following:

Driest parts are Porth Neigwl (*Hell's Mouth*), Aberdaron and the northern coast, and Pwllheli.

Wettest parts – East of a line from Nefyn to Cricieth is wetter than the west, with the edge of the mountains being significantly wetter.

Sunniest parts are Aberdaron and Penrhyn Cilan (Abersoch), with the area east of a line from Trefor to Porthmadog being noticeably less sunny.

Warmest – The whole of the southern coast is warmer, especially Pwllheli and Porthmadog, plus an area around Nefyn. It is noticeably cooler around the end (Aberdaron) and Yr Eifl (Llithfaen-Trefor).

Rain – On average Llŷn receives only 36 inches of rain per annum, with half of this falling between October and February. Statistically, March to June are the driest months.

Wind – Aberdaron is particularly exposed to the wind, and very wild winds are not unknown. In December 1997 there was a recorded gust of 112 mph. You can find a wonderful website for wind forecasts, hour by hour, 8 days ahead, at www.windfinder.com, with forecasts for Aberdaron, Cricieth and Trefor.

The Clouds – Above your head a weather forecast is unfolding minute by minute, in the form of the cloud movement and patterns, at different layers of the atmosphere. To help you interpret these changes you could do worse than to read Gavin Pretor-Pinny The Cloudspotter's Guide.

The Railways

Arriva Trains Wales

Reservations to carry bicycles on trains are required on the Pwllheli-Shrewsbury line, and on the Chester-Bangor-Holyhead line, with a limit of 2 bikes per train. Reservations are not required on the Llandudno Junction-Blaenau Ffestiniog line, with bikes carried free subject to space being available.

Arriva Trains Wales has the rail franchise on these lines until 2018. The Company was taken over in August 2010 by Deutsche Bahn, the German railway company.

Welsh Highland and Ffestiniog Railways

www.welshhighlandrailway.net
www.ffestiniograilway.co.uk

The Ffestiniog Railway runs up to Blaenau Ffestiniog from Porthmadog. There is limited accommodation for bicycles. It operated commercially from 1832 to 1946 and re-opened shortly after for passengers.

The Welsh Highland Railway, in contrast, was a huge commercial white elephant, opening in 1922 and operating for just 15 years. Restoration began in the 1960's, and the line will be fully opened, from Caernarfon through Beddgelert to the Harbour Station in Porthmadog in April 2011. Bicycle wagons will be attached to most trains.

Ynys Enlli (*Bardsey*)

What do you do when you're digging up your potatoes and up come human bones? On the mainland the police are informed, on Ynys Enlli you dig them back in, for they are probably the bones of saints, possibly even Saint David himself. According to the early C12th Book of Llandaf, 20,000 (a ballpark figure) saints were buried here, and in medieval times the island was known as Ynys y Saint (*the Island of the Saints*). Ynys Enlli can be translated as the *island in the tempestuous, treacherous waters*. *Bard'r* was the name of a Viking chieftain, and *sea* is Norse for 'island'.

Day trips to Ynys Enlli are still weather dependent. For up-to-date information contact Colin Evans (tel. 07971 769895 www.bardseyboattrips.com or 07836 293146 www.enllicharter.co.uk). One working farm remains, and the lighthouse still operates, built in 1821, though it is now automated. Others live on the island for long periods of the year: Earnest, Colin's father, is the postman and a fisherman, Emyr is the resident Trust manager. Accommodation is available to rent, through the Bardsey Island Trust (www.bardsey.org), and the Bardsey Bird and Field Observatory. It was designated a National Nature Reserve in 1986, around 8,000 birds are ringed each year, and it is otherwise known for the grey seals and the

Puffins on Llŷn's shoreline

Manx shearwaters. Around 16,000 pairs come here to lay and incubate their eggs in abandoned rabbit holes or newly dug holes. Each year they fly 12,000km to and from their wintering grounds in South America. The best all-round book to read is *Bardsey* by Christine Evans, Gomer Press, 2008.

There is evidence of human occupation on Ynys Enlli from Mesolithic times (7-9,000 years ago), but it was during the great Christian awakening from around AD 450 and for the next couple of hundred years, that Ynys Enlli, along with other islands such as Iona and Lindisfarne, attracted those seeking a place of peace to worship. St Cadfan was the first Abbot, having arrived from Brittany about 516. According to tradition, the first Bishop of Bangor, Deiniol, was buried here in 584, and monks fled here from their monastery at Bangor Iscoed in the Dee Valley near Chester after a massacre of the holy men by Saxons in 616. Shortly after AD 1100 the Augustinian Canons established an abbey on the island.

Forgiveness and healing were sought by these early Christians in places believed to have special spirituality, and thus began the journeys known as pilgrimages. The Book of Llandaf refers to Ynys Enlli as the Rome of Britain, stressing the length and danger of the journey as well as the island's sanctity and purity.

By 1533, when Henry VIII began the Dissolution of the

The ruins of the abbey on Bardsey

Bottlenose dolphin and an
Atlantic greyseal in Bae Cerdigion

Monasteries, the Abbey buildings were empty, and all that remains today is the tower within a more recent cemetery. In 1537 it became Crown property, and was given, in 1553 to Sion Wyn ap Huw of Bodfel, Llannor. The island was thriving, nonetheless, as a port of call for pirates. It was alleged that all the local squires, including justices and the sheriff, were only too happy to use their services. All, that is, except Siôn Gruffydd of Cefnamwlch (d. 1584) who tried to bring them to justice, even as his own brother-in-law, the aforesaid Siôn Wyn ap Huw of Bodfel kept a servant on Ynys Enlli to provide a supply of food for the visitors in exchange for wine, iron, salt and spices.

Later a farming and fishing community grew here, and by the early C20th, 90 people lived on the island, growing barley, eating seagull's eggs, fishing and selling rabbit skins and dairy produce by delivering them in boats to Liverpool. The landlord at the time, Lord Newborough, appointed an islander with the title 'King' to settle disputes and collect the rents. The last was Love Pritchard who died in 1926.

Marine Conservation

Since 2004 much of the coast and inshore waters of Llŷn have been designated a Special Area of Conservation (SAC) (www.penllynarsarau.com).

It is the second largest SAC in the country and covers 230 km of coastline from Nefyn down to Aberystwyth including the seas around Ynys Enlli (Bardsey), and the whole of the northern Bae Ceredigion (*Cardigan Bay*). It is called *Pen Llŷn a'r Sarnau SAC*.

These waters have a huge variety of marine life, from 10m long basking sharks and conger eels to flat fish and sea mice, and the habitats include reefs and caves (St Tudwals Islands have caves containing ledges used by seals as sleeping platforms), estuaries, salt marsh and mud flats. In 2009 sightings included the Portuguese Man o'War, a jellyfish with 30m long tentacles capable of giving a really painful sting.

There are probably about 1,000 grey seals in the SAC. Not much is known about them, but they can often be spotted bobbing in the water or at haul-out sites from Ynys Enlli to Morfa Nefyn. It contains one of the two main UK semi-resident populations of bottlenose dolphin, mainly in Bae Ceredigion, but they have been spotted all over the SAC. Estimates of numbers vary from 130 to 350. Unfortunately they are adversely affected by the increasing numbers of power craft around the coast.

The designation will help to protect and manage life in the seas, and also to educate us. The regular programme of events includes wildlife walks, kayak safaris and active projects such as beach cleanups.

Fishing

Sitting virtually in the middle of the Irish Sea, Llŷn picks up the movement of large currents of water – warm Gulf Stream currents from the south through the Celtic Sea, and cold from the north

A Llŷn fisherman launching his boat at Porth Meudwy

through the North Channel. As any swimmer will testify, there is often a noticeable difference in water temperature between the northern and southern coasts of Llŷn. These two currents mix in the Irish Sea, and where they come together high densities of plankton are brought to the surface, attracting fish and plankton eating mammals such as the basking shark. As a consequence sea angling is popular, with a good variety in the summer months, though there are times when, as a neighbour put it, all I'm doing is sitting in the sun for a while.

As a cyclist much of this will pass you by, except that from the shore you can often watch terns diving vertically into the sea searching for fish, and, a little further out, northern gannets spectacularly plunge down into the water to hunt. These birds are the largest sea birds in the North Atlantic, with a wingspan approaching 2 m. They can dive from heights of 30 m, and reach speeds of 100 km/hour.

The problem is that above plankton on the food chain are sand eels. They move in large numbers, and when they are around it can seem as if the sea were boiling. Porpoises, seal and dolphin rely on sand eels, as do puffins and guillemots and many other species of fish and sea birds. But the fishing of sand eels is not regulated and they are targeted by industrial 'Hoover' fishing and used on the fields of Russia as fertiliser or as fish food for farmed fish.

Rocks and Metals

I am no geologist. I know more about rhubarb than what lies beneath my feet, but we see rock every day, and if there were no hard crust on the Earth we'd be in a bit of a pickle. Technically clay and peat are rock formed recently and on their way to something else. The following timeline should give you some idea of when the rock on Llŷn was formed. There are roughly two types of rock, sedimentary, rock that was formed by the hardening of sediments accumulating on the bottom of seas or other stretches of water, and igneous, rock formed when a mass of hot, molten material pushes towards the crust and cools. It doesn't have to have reached the surface, but may well be exposed by subsequent erosion.

Timeline

2008 AD   A recent Grand Slam win for Wales
10,000 years ago   End of the last Ice Age
120-150 million years ago (Jurassic period) Dinosaurs roamed
220-280 million years ago (Carboniferous) Coal measures laid down
280-320 million years ago (Devonian) Fish swam in the sea
320-350 million years ago (Silurian)
350-400 million years ago (Ordovician)
400-500 million years ago (Cambrian) A whole variety of sea

creatures call trilobites were the dominant life force 500+ million years ago (Pre-Cambrian)

You want old rocks? We've got old rocks. Some very old Pre-Cambrian sedimentary schist and gneiss run westwards from Nefyn along the northern coast to Mynydd Mawr, some of the oldest rock in Britain, and in contrast, Yr Eifl (the Rivals), Garn Fadryn and Garn Boduan are Ordovician granite intrusions pushed up into a sea of Ordovician sedimentary rock.

Rocks, Minerals and Metals of value

1 Jasper has been quarried on Mynydd Carreg. It is an impure silica, usually cherry red here in Llŷn, with variegated pieces running through it, which polishes up as a gemstone. Jasper from Mynydd Carreg can be seen in Westminster Abbey.

2 Slate. In central Gwynedd, including Nantlle and Cwm Pennant, the slate beds are Cambrian. Mud, pebbles and sand collected on the seabed a mile down. Volcanoes erupted and the resulting granites covered the slate to a depth of 7,600 m. Pressure compressed the slate further and then folded and twisted the layers of rock. The main slate quarrying areas were to the south of Llŷn, around Blaenau Ffestiniog, and to the east of Porthmadog at Croesor, Bethesda, Llanberis and Nantlle.

3 Manganese ("Mango"). In the early days (mid C19th) the manganese found at Rhiw was used in the production of bleach, paint and varnish, and the making and handling of glass, as it had a high percentage of silica (30% manganese, 2% iron, 24% silica), but towards the end of C19th it was used in the smelting process to toughen and harden steel and give it a longer life, which

proven most useful in the making of rails, armaments, ships and machinery.

4   The Metals. On the Cilan peninsula, at Llanengan near Porth Neigwl (*Hell's Mouth*), and Penrhyn Du, *south* of Abersoch, metals were found. The first finds date from the 1630's when Thomas Bushell, lessor of the Mines Royal in northern Wales, was scouring the Principality for silver to be made into coins at the Royal Mint in Aberystwyth. Also found were the ores of iron, manganese and copper, but it was the lead which proved the most valuable, and lead ore was mined here for the next 250 years.

5   Granite. To the south and east of Nefyn, the Pre-Cambrian igneous rocks are of a type of granite called porphyry and syenite. All along this coast granite was quarried, essentially for 'setts', squarish stones used to pave roads, and then, with the introduction of stone crushing machines, the quarries produced road stone, railway ballast and concrete aggregates. The large quarry at Trefor produced setts and chippings , and operated from 1850 to 1971. It also produced stones for curling, and the British team of Scotswomen in the 2002 Winter Olympics won the curling gold medal with stones from Trefor.

6   Flints, Arrows and Axes. Flints and arrowheads have been found in Llŷn, probably left behind by primitive Mesolithic nomadic hunter-gatherers who penetrated the area about 8,000-4,000 BC. Stone axes and mace heads were tools used by Neolithic farmers, the first settled agricultural communities, from 4,000-2,000 BC. The stone axe factory on Mynydd Rhiw dates from approximately 2,500-2,000 BC.

The chough, on a cliff ledge – and also on the logo of AONB Llŷn

The Chough

In Welsh, *brân goesgoch*, the 'red-legged crow'.

Once common in the British Isles, this bird is now a rarity, but there are about 1,000 breeding pairs in Llŷn.

I.D. black plumage; curved red bill; red legs. In flight choughs are spectacular performers, doing acrobatics like a raven, with their wing feathers splayed in 6 'fingers'. Their call is a harsh 'k chuf' or an unmusical 'kree-aw'. Apparently, the courtship is lovely, with strutting, flapping, caressing, preening and acrobatic waltzing. Apparently.

The Diving Birds

The ones nearer the shore are tern, probably common tern, the 'swallows of the sea', with their forked tails. They hover, then acrobatically plunge into the sea after their small fish prey.

Further out to sea are gannet. With a wingspan of up to six feet, the gannet glides over the sea. When they fish, they dive-bomb their catch from up to a hundred feet up with wings folded back to form a living arrowhead.

Welsh Names

My name has 2 parts. 'Philip' was plucked from the air by my Mum and Dad before I was born. Being of good Socialist mining stock, they have consistently denied it had anything to do with Phil the Greek, the young husband of the future Queen, or Philip the Handsome (C15th King of Castile) or even Philip the Good (C15th Duke of Burgundy). 'Horsley' will be Old English (i.e. Anglo-Saxon C5th to mid C11th), from *leah*, a wood or a glade, and the horse. The Anglo-Saxons also assimilated older British or Celtic names when they came into contact, but the language spoken out here is Brythonic Welsh, i.e. related to the old languages of Cornwall and Brittany, and the names are Celtic, and patronymic. For example the publisher's name is Myrddin ap (*son of*) Dafydd. The female equivalent is 'ferch' (daughter of), e.g. Gwen ferch Ieuan.

Anglicisation of names was common in Norman lands and the Welsh Borders from C14th, but not out here. During the reign of Henry VIII surnames became hereditary for the gentry as an important way of establishing title to property, and this practise slowly spread into the ordinary people. After the Act of Union 1536, the welsh language was exiled from official circles and the Welsh people were supposed to adopt English-type fixed hereditary surnames. These names reflect their patronymic heritage, i.e. Jones (John's son), Thomas, Williams, Davies. Some even contain the prefix, e.g. Pritchard (ap Richard), Bowen (ap(b) Owen).

In practise, I am known locally after the name of my house, i.e. Phil Ty'n Parc.

Welsh

Together with the Hebrides and the Channel Islands, this is the only bilingual part of the UK. Welsh is the language of Llŷn. All the native local people speak Welsh most of the time. Virtually all schooling is in Welsh. But the vast majority of locals are bilingual. There is no need to point or shout, they will understand you. A few of the older locals find English difficult, the pronunciation, the vocabulary, the spelling but mostly the peculiar way we construct our sentences. It is worth remembering that it is an entirely separate language, you speak one and you speak the other, there is no such thing as Franglais in Welsh.

Welsh, or Old Welsh, and it's ancestor 'Brythoneg' or 'Britannic' was the language spoken over most of the territory of Britain until around 400 AD, until the invasions began and other languages became dominant. Unfortunately, from 1536 until around 1900, English became the only language of law and administration, and state education in Wales, and the main language of commerce. Welsh was banned from schools in C19th. Since the 1960's Welsh has seen a resurgence.

In 1991, 75% of Llŷn dwellers could speak Welsh (compared to 21% for the whole of Wales), though the influx of non-Welsh speakers since then has reduced this percentage. We are encouraged to learn the language. The community newspaper, *Llanw Llŷn* began in 1977 and sells 2,000 a month.

If you go to the theatre or other entertainment it will say whether it is in English or Welsh. Expect the numbers on the raffle tickets to be called in Welsh.

Unfortunately I do not yet speak Welsh. I love listening to the language, it is a spoken, lyrical language. It mutates.

You need to be able to not panic when faced with Welsh place names. The book to read is *Pronouncing Welsh Place-names* by Tony Leaver (Gwasg Carreg Gwalch), but here are some really simple rules:

– Don't panic
– Break down the word into components
  e.g. Garndolbenmaen Garn_dol_ben_maen
  Llanystumdwy Llan_y_stum_dwy
– As a general rule pronounce every letter, with the stress on
  the next to the last syllable. Unlike English, Welsh is a phonetic
  language i.e. each letter is always pronounced in the same
  way.
– The consonants.
– As English except
  'c' is always hard (as in come)
  'g' is always hard (a in goal)
  'r' is trilled
  'rh' is trilled
  'dd' is pronounced 'th'
  'f' is pronounced 'v'
  'ff' is pronounced 'f' (as in daffodil)
  'ch' is pronounced as in the Scottish 'loch', or the German
  'bach'
  'll' is pronounced by blowing voicelessly with your tongue in
the roof of your mouth. I recently came across a C20th English
aristocrat whose name was Flewellyn, which helped his fellow
grouse-shooters to pronounce his name.

The vowels are more tricky. There are 7, a e i o u w y. The first four
can be pronounced short or long, but mainly are short.
  'w' is pronounced 'u' as in pull, or longer as in the 'oo' in fool
  'y' is pronounced 'i' as in pin
  'u' is pronounced as a rounded 'i' or 'ee'.

Finally, as a visitor, it will help to know some common words;

diolch	thanks
diolch yn fawr	thank you
bore da	good morning
p'nawn da	good afternoon
noswaith dda	good evening
nos dawch	good night
iawn	ok
ta ta/hwyl!	bye
plis	please
peint o gwrw	pint of beer
iechyd da	good health
beic	bicycle
llwybr beicio	cycle path
tafarn	pub
lle tea	tea room
dynion	mens (toilet)
merched	ladies (toilet)
maes parcio	car park
gwely a brecwast	bed and breakfast
trên	train
siop	shop
traeth	beach
gwesty	hotel
afon	river
eglwys	church
heddlu	police.

The Enclosures

When Thomas Pennant journeyed through northern Wales in the 1770's he considered the rural part of Llŷn to be a backwater. 'The houses of the common people are very mean; made with clay, thatched and destitute of chimneys.' The land was undeveloped and used for the grazing of Welsh Black cattle, and 'neglected for the sake of the herring-fishery.' From Nefyn alone, 5,000 barrels of herring a year were exported in 1747.

Several thousand head of black cattle a year were sold to markets in England. The droving routes were mainly off-road, and began at fairs, markets or smithies, for example at Sarn, Botwnnog, Rhydyclafdy, Efailnewydd and Y Ffôr.

Walter Davies, writing in 1810, described the houses as made of turf or clay, roofed with poles covered with heath or rushes kept down by ropes, through which the smoke from the peat fire filtered. Openings in the wall were filled with a lattice of sticks, and a hurdle for a door . . . a greater part of . . . Caernarfon is disgraced with a species of cottages which are truly the habitations of wretchedness; one smoky hearth, for it should not be styled a kitchen; one damp litter-cell for it cannot be called a bedroom . . . (is) frequently all the space allotted to a labourer, his wife and four or five children.'

By this time the Enclosures had begun, large landowners obtaining Acts of Parliament to enclose common and waste ground.

The first was in 1802, two or three thousand acres of Rhoshirwaun commons. The commons were wet and boggy but local people had grazing rights and the right to gather peat for fuel. Many had squatted here, exercising their traditional right of Hywel Dda, the process of building a turf cottage overnight, and have smoke rising from the Hafod Unnos, or Tŷ Unnos (*Moonlight Cottages*) by the morning. In places a compromise was reached, and those hasty dwellings which had been there for twenty years or more were allowed to stay or bought off, the rest were destroyed.

Other areas followed, 4,000 acres to the west of Pwllheli in 1808, and in 1812, 10,000 acres between Nefyn and Llanllyfni, the main beneficiaries being Lord Newborough of Glynllifon and

Richard Edwards of Nanhoron.

The dispossessed were incensed and fought the changes. In September 1812 the Clerk to the Commissioners was pelted with stones and clods of earth. The dragoons were summoned. Two of the ringleaders from the protestors to the Rhoshirwaun clearances were transported to Australia, and in 1813, a man from Cae'r Mynydd, Llithfaen was sent to Botany Bay.

The newly enclosed land was parcelled out in regular fields, and new straight roads built. Field boundaries were made of piled up earth topped with a hedge, quick thorn, hawthorn or gorse. (Barbed wire was not invented until1870). Substantial farmhouses often followed, and these can easily be picked out today often sited on a rise. This is essentially the landscape you see today. But many of the humble dwellings remain, low and rectangular, their walls cement rendered and re-roofed in slate. I'm typing this in one now, the yard outside cobbled with beach stones. Others

Cae'r Mynydd, Llithfaen

have been let go, their clay walls still standing, decaying only slowly back into the fields from which they came. At the beginning of the C20th there were three dwellings close to this one, they are marked on the map, and their inhabitants named and described in the Census. All have completely disappeared. But the most significant change in the last few years has been the use of the buildings in the village. In this scattered village of Llangwnnadl, with it's two builders, caravan sites, bee keeper, internet salesman, airline purser, handful of farms, a small group of other wage earners and retired folk, at least a half of the houses are second homes or holiday lets. According to the 1892 Census these 57 houses were occupied by:-

- a threshing machine driver
- a coal and manure merchant
- a cattle and butter merchant
- a drover
- 3 joiners
- 2 carpenters
- a smith
- a tailor apprentice
- 3 dressmakers
- a schoolmaster
- a clerk of holy orders
- a carrier
- a shoemaker
- 2 shopkeepers
- 78 farmers or farm labourers
- 6 sailors or mariners
- 2 miners
- 20 domestic servants
- 6 parish paupers

The church remains, and one of the chapels, but the shop, a chapel and school have closed. Note – there is no mention of a pub!

The Gentry

From the C17th to the C19th several large estates dominated Llŷn, with the gentry further extending their influence by filling the positions of High Sheriff and Justice of the Peace. In the first half of the C19th just four landlords held 50% of the land in Llŷn proper: Richard Lloyd Edward's Nanhoron Estate; Charles Wynne Griffith-Wynne of Cefnamwlch; Sir Love Parry Jones Parry's Madryn Estate; and Lord Newborough's Estate centred on Boduan. In addition the holdings of Thomas Assheton Smith's Faenol Estate; Douglas Pennant's Penrhyn Estate and Edward Lloyd of Mostyn (Llandudno) were also considerable. In Arfon the Faenol Estate and Lord Newborough of Glynllifon dominated, and in Eifionydd there were a number of smaller estates, Gwynfryn, and Clenennau for example, with Talhenbont becoming the largest through marriage and acquisition.

These great Estates had their origins in the control exercised by the feudal Princes. Through intermarriage a class of landed gentry grew in power, fuelled by the wealth generated by mineral extraction.

Chapel

You don't travel far in Llŷn without passing a chapel. Although many have been converted to private dwellings, their shape is distinctive. Why were so many built within such a relatively short time span, and who paid for them? Llŷn has never been awash with spare cash.

For an answer, we could begin with King Charles I. His Dad, James I (James VI of Scotland), it was said, had 'a genius for getting

Capel Nanhoran (Capel Newydd)

into difficulties', but 'if he steered the ship straight for the rocks, he left his son to wreck it'. (G Watkin). Charles believed in the 'Divine Right' of Kings, which eventually led to civil war and his own beheading in 1649.The Nonconformist churches grew from the politics of the subsequent Parliament, and the Parliamentary party of the Presbyterians, but it was not until 1689 and the Act of Toleration that freedom was granted to build licensed meeting houses.

In Llŷn the Anglican church, supported by the gentry, was still dominant in 1800, though there were groups of fervent Independents in Pwllheli, Llangybi and Llangian (Capel Newydd was built in 1769). Then, in the 30 years to 1836 there was an explosion in Nonconformist membership, and again, at the turn of the Century, a series of religious revivals led to a renewal of chapel building. Financially they were self-supporting, built with money raised locally from working people. Use was made of builders catalogues for both internal and external work, and the arrival of the railways (Pwllheli 1867) made mass production economic.

The chapels were not of one single religious organisation, but of different movements, made more complicated by divisions and re-unifications.

The early dissenters in Wales were Congregationalists (or Independents). They originated in Mary's reign when they met as secret 'congregations', and thrived under Cromwell. Each Congregation is autonomous and responsible for the life and mission of it's church.

Also originating in the Presbyterians were the Calvinists (or Particular Baptists). They organised around a church government of elected elders; ministers and certain laymen, of equal rank, from each congregation, who enforced a strict code of ethics. The chapels were also used as schools. As they grew in number larger buildings were required. The 1875 Calvinist Chapel in Nefyn seated over 1,000. It has since been demolished.

The General Baptists (or Arminium) were opposed to Calvin's doctrine of predestination, i.e. the idea that certain souls (the elect) are predestined by God through the sacrifice of Jesus to salvation, and the rest of us to damnation. The first Baptist missionaries arrived on Llŷn in 1776.

Arminism is also the basis of the Wesleyan Methodists. About 1739 John and Charles Wesley met together with other Oxford students, at fixed times to pray and study the bible. The term 'Methodist' was originally derisory due to their excessive adherence to strict rules and methods.

It has been argued that the Nonconformists were a powerful influence in the preservation of the Welsh language, and their moral leadership was much needed. Attendances at chapel were huge. In 1851 the combined average weekly attendance at Sunday services in Nefyn alone was 2,347.

Chapel Part 2

In 1851 the combined average attendances at Sunday services in Nefyn was 2,347 (according to Roland Bond, *The Story of an Ancient Gwynedd Town and Parish*, Gwasg Carreg Gwalch, 2008, a wonderful book). By the turn of the Century a further 8 chapels had been built in the surrounding settlements, and the Calvinist Methodist chapel built in 1875 could seat over 1,000. Why? Every few miles, all over Llŷn a chapel has been built. Why was the movement so strong?

At the beginning of C19th the established church retained it's historic commitment to a rural society presided over by the landed gentry. The parson himself was part of 'society'. Throughout England and Wales there was unrest and dissent, a feeling that the new wealth of the mill owners, the mine owners, the landed gentry with their 'enclosures' was being created on the back of the exploited and impoverished worker. The gentry could afford a Regency home in London. the worker faced 14 hours of back-breaking work every day. This dissent found a natural focus in the chapel. Fired by a passion and religious zeal, the poor set about improving their lot. 'Welsh is their language and democratic is their ethos, the different denominations were united by their dogged struggle against the privileges and power of the predominantly Anglicised and Conservative Church of England.' (Hughes and O'Leary, *Wales of One Hundred Years Ago*).

So the chapel, firstly, was Welsh, not English. There was a real fear that the language was dying. Schooling was in English. As a child you learned to read and write your own language only at Sunday school with the bible. Equally as important, chapels were self managed. Making a living on Llŷn was often precarious and the people learned mutual self-reliance. Why not extend this to the place of worship as well. I can imagine that they quickly became social and community centres too, places to meet and learn (certainly later on, when the women could become involved). Plus, you could raise the roof in song, in Welsh. The money to build and to furnish all the chapels you see was raised locally by poor, ordinary folk.

From 1875 to 1939, with only a brief respite around the 1914-1918 War, British agriculture was in a state of chronic depression. There was always the need to find money to pay rent, so the best was sold, and work/labour occupied virtually all available hours, in the fields or as a servant. The religious revival of 1904/5 under the leadership of Evan Roberts appealed especially to women and young people, the two main groups in society marginalised by organised religion. But it was short-lived, the light of Nonconformity was beginning to dim. Around this time the writings of Caradoc Evans depicted life as a brutalising experience in which the adherents to the Nonconformist were complicit, a direct challenge to the chapels, which thought of themselves as a cultural haven cocooned from the worst elements of modern life. And that modern life was beginning to include temptations. By 1900 thousands of strangers from Lancashire and the Midlands reached as far as Pwllheli and Nefyn for holidays by the sea. They brought with them money to spend, and they also attracted entertainment, fairs, donkeys, singing and dancing.

David Lloyd George must have been an influential figure here on Llŷn, perhaps even a 'celebrity'. From his Nonconformist background he had acquired the ability to communicate, his speeches using a series of pictures and metaphors, but it could be that his influence benefited Liberal politics at the expense of the chapel. Liberal, note, not Socialist, there is little evidence on Llŷn of the institutions which I grew up with, the Working Mens Clubs, Institutes, and Libraries.

Attendances at chapel are as poor nowadays as for the Anglican Church, apart from weddings and funerals, but their influence could be felt here as late as 1996, when Dwyfor was one of the last places in which people voted to allow the sale of alcohol on a Sunday.

William Alexander Madocks

The price of roofing slates doubled between 1798 and 1825 as demand soared. The Ffestiniog quarries produced thousands of tons of slates, but to get them to the industrial towns, they began their journey on pack animals, transferring firstly to small boats on Afon Dwyrd in the Vale of Ffestiniog, and then onto larger ships off the sand dunes between Borthygest and Morfa Bychan.

In addition, the journey from Llŷn to England began with the crossing of Traeth Mawr, near Porthmadog, and this was almost as much of a problem as the crossing of the Menai Strait further north. Pennant says it was a 'most dangerous passage to strangers, by reason of the tides which flow here with great rapidity.'

The Act of Union with Ireland in 1801 meant Irish M.P.'s travelling regularly to Westminster, and pressure grew on the Government to improve the passage across the Irish Sea. The Porth Dinllaen Harbour Company was formed in 1806, and a Bill presented to Parliament to fund a harbour at Porth Dinllaen, which also meant that the crossing of Traeth Mawr required improvement.

William Alexander Madocks was a London lawyer with estates in Wales. He was already buying land around Penmorfa for agricultural improvement as the Enclosure Acts were passed, and he had nibbled into Traeth Mawr with an embankment (which can still be seen) from Prenteg to Porthmadog. Behind this he built a small town in an C18th style and called it Tremadog, on a spot which traditionally was the starting point of the C12th Welsh explorer Prince Madog, who was said to have been one of the first

Traeth Mawr Minffordd, before the Porthmadog Cob was built

to reach America. Madocks improved the house at Tan yr Allt and moved in. One of his neighbours was the infant Lawrence of Arabia, born in Tremadog in August 1808 (there is a plaque).

Built as a model town, Madocks expressed his ambition by naming the main street Dublin Street. The 1810 Parliamentary Committee had, as it's brief, a review of the route from London to Ireland. It was inconclusive, and met again the following year, this time with Thomas Telford presenting a report, and this time the proposal to make Porth Dinllaen the ferry terminal to Ireland was defeated by one vote in favour of Holyhead, with a Telford designed road through the mountains and a bridge across the Menai Strait.

The great embankment, the Cob, was finished in July 1811 at an astronomical cost of £60,000. Madocks was now in debt, compounded by repairs to a breach in February 1812, and he was forced to transfer his lands to other ownerships and let them to his main creditor. It was about this time that the 19 year old Percy Bysshe Shelley and his young wife came to help, and became tenants of Tan yr Allt. Shelley did himself no favours by criticizing the locals for growing sheep to eat, and by not paying any of his local debts. They departed suddenly following an apparent attack. Meanwhile Madocks' finances improved dramatically through a fortunate marriage, and he was able to re-acquire his holdings, build a railway on top of the embankment and the quays of Porthmadog. He died in September 1828.

The diversion of the Afon Glaslyn carved out a deep channel, which was eminently suitable as a harbour. The railway up to Ffestiniog was largely the work of Samuel Holland and was completed in 1836 at a cost of £6,000. The locals were opposed as it bypassed all the local porterage.

The town boomed as the slate quarries boomed. Ffestiniog slate was shipped to Australia and to America, and Hamburg is almost entirely roofed with slate shipped out of Porthmadog. At it's peak, in 1873, the town exported 116,567 tons of slate, but after the turn of the Century the boom times were over, and the Great War severed all trade with Germany.

Moving around Llŷn

The first proper road was the Roman one from Segontium, near Caernarfon, South through Dolbenmaen to Porthmadog, but then Llŷn had to wait until the late C18th when a turnpike was built from Caernarfon to Clynnog, Llanaelhaearn and Pwllheli (the A499), and in the first part of C19th other turnpikes followed, to Porth Dinllaen (the B4354 from Cricieth, and the A497 from Pwllheli). At about the same time many of the drovers roads, and especially the marshy tracks towards Aberdaron and in the Pwllheli/Llanbedrog area, were improved with the enclosures. But the easiest way to move around Llŷn was by sea.

Small boats were still using the coves and beaches of Llŷn well into the 1930's. Local agricultural produce, butter, cheese, eggs, chickens and pigs were exported, particularly to Liverpool, and fish too, especially from Nefyn.

Incoming cargoes, from Caernarfon and Liverpool, included iron and bricks, lemons and tar, tobacco, wood and crockery, but the main commodities were lime, for mortar and to lower the acidity of the soil in the fields (many of the harbours and coves had lime kilns, like those remaining at Porth Ysgadan and Porth Golmon), and coal. Coal merchants delivered by boat to just about every cove on Llŷn, unloading straight from the boats to waiting carts while the tide was out.

The boats used were sloops, ketch and small brigs, one or two masted, flat bottomed, snub nosed, perhaps 60 feet long, carrying cargoes of up to 100 tons. In good weather the journey to Liverpool took 3 or 4 days. Most of the coastal farms had a track down to the shore , for incoming goods, for the collection of seaweed for the fields and stones for the walls and paths, and for access to the small boat kept on the shore to fish from.

See www.rhiw.com

Glossary of Biblical names of chapels.

Beersheba The Seventh largest city in Israel. Features throughout the Old Testament, with numerous comings and goings.

Berea The ancient city of Beroea, now known as Veria, or Veroia. It is a small Macedonian city north of Mount Olympus, where Paul of Tarsus preached and where the people examined the scriptures to see if his preaching was true.

Bethania Bethania is a village on the Mount of Olives. Jesus parted from his disciples here at the Ascension.

Bethel   The place where Jacob dreams of a ladder stretching between Heaven and Earth, thronged with angels.

Carmel   A mountain in Palestine.

Ebenezer   A Hebrew name meaning 'stone of the help'.

Gerizim   Mount Gerizim, 881m, (2849feet), near Nablus, is one of the highest peaks in the West Bank. It is the sacred mountain of the Samaritan religion.

Golan   Golan Heights, a plateau on the Syrian/ Israeli border, annexed by Israel in 1981.

Hebron   The second largest city in the West Bank, and second holiest place of Judaism after Jerusalem, being the burial place of Abraham and Sarah, Isaac and Rebecca, Jacob and Leah, the fathers and mothers of the Jewish people.

Horeb   Hebrew name of a mountain, probably Mount Sinai, where Moses received the Ten Commandments. 'Horeb' means the Sun, 'Sinai' means the Moon.

Libanus   Ancient name for Mount Lebanon, home of the Cedars of Lebanon. King Hiram I of Tyre sent some Cedar wood (and engineers) to build the Jewish temple of Jerusalem.

Moreia   Unlikely to refer to the Mexican drugs town, the Majorcan resort or the 4 metre long sea eels. More likely to be the Welsh for Moriah.

Moriah   The mountain, as mentioned in Genesis, on which the sacrifice of Isaac was to take place by his father Abraham.

Nasareth   Town in Galilee, population approx. 80,000. Boyhood home of Jesus.

Nebo   The Chaldean deity of the Babylonians and Assyrians.

Peniel   Here Jacob wrestled with the angels (i.e. God), 'til the break of day'. The scene has been painted by Rembrandt, Delacroix, Gauguin and Marc Chagall among others.

Salem chapel at Pwllheli

Pisgah The mountain from which Moses saw the Promised Land for the first time.

Salem Mentioned in Genesis, Salem is a shorter form of Jerusalem.

Sardis In present day Turkey. Sardis was one of the great pre-Christian cities of Asia Minor. It is famous for it's synagogue.

Saron, or Sharon The largest city in Netanya in Israel. The plain was particularly fertile and prosperous in ancient times.

Seion Zion in English. Hebrew name for Jerusalem or the Promise Land.

Siloh (English – Shiloh) Was the assembly place for the people of Israel. It was a sanctuary containing the Ark of the Covenant. Now a Jewish village with a grocery store, swimming pool and replica of the Biblical Tabernacle.

Soar   Not the Southern Astrophysical Research Telescope
             in Chile, nor the GP's reference directory, the Scottish
             Online Appraisal Resources, but a reference to Isaiah
             40 v 31 'They will soar on wings like eagles.'

Electricity

Arguably the most important change on Llŷn was the arrival of
electricity. There is no coal here, so no town gas or street lighting.
Heating was peat or wood or, more usually imported coal. Lighting
was by paraffin lamp. Radios were powered by large wet batteries,
and their use strictly controlled by parents because charging was
awkward and expensive. Electricity reached much of Llŷn only in the
1950's and 1960's. Imagine not hearing the Beatles until Sergeant
Pepper.

The irony is that on the flanks of Snowdon, the Cwm Dyli hydro-
electric power station, built in 1905, is Britain's oldest operating
power station. It was built by a railway company, the plan being
to build a network of narrow gauge electric railway lines around
Snowdonia, but it was never completed, and all that remains is
the Welsh Highland Line. Instead the station provided power for
the quarries at Blaenau Ffestiniog, Llanberis and Nantlle, the lines
being carried through the mountains on wooden poles. Bear in
mind that this was untried technology back then, and no-one
knew whether the poles would stand up in a Snowdonia winter.
Construction involved 800 men using horses and steam traction
engines. By 1918 the line was extended to the quarries around
Nefyn, and on to Waunfawr to power Marconi's Long Wave Wireless
Telegraph transmitter, part of the first transatlantic wireless
service. In 1928 new hydro-electric plants were built at Maentwrog
and Dolgarrog, and power lines extended to Cricieth and Pwllheli.

After nationalisation in 1948 the CEGB standardised the
generating systems and set about building networks of power

supply. Basically, Llŷn is served from Four Crosses (Y Ffôr) with loops and spurs going out from there. There are a handful only of metal pylons in Llŷn (apart from the high voltage line which skirts the mountains and which was built to connect the new nuclear power station at Trawsffynydd to the grid) and thousands of wooden poles. These are European spruce soaked in creosote and are expected to last around 40 years. British spruce was tried but the poles tended to snap. The main problem is woodpeckers, which bore holes in the wood, penetrating the heartwood, water gets in and they rot from the inside. Poles can last a long time though. Only recently have some of the original 1908 poles been replaced, having withstood almost a hundred Snowdonia winters.

The system is being computerised, with automatic switching and faults being detected remotely. Manweb were taken over by Scottish Power, which in turn was swallowed by the Spanish Iberdrola, and that is a target for the huge French and German companies. The local man is Bill Nottingham, the man who opened my eyes to electricity in Llŷn.

Water

In 1945 Caernarfonshire County Council commissioned a report on the state of the supply of drinking water. It painted a sorry picture of corroded cast iron and asbestos cement pipes carrying unfiltered, untreated and sometimes polluted water from springs and small streams liable to dry up in summer. And only 45% of the houses had piped water, the rest used wells or carried water from streams. There was at least one unconfirmed report of cadmium pollution from groundwater causing a serious health hazard.

In the early 1950's Llŷn Rural District Council built a direct supply reservoir at Cwmystradllyn and began the job of laying new pipelines throughout Llŷn.

At the other end, in the last fifteen years or so improvements have been made so that all sewage is fully treated before discharge. Before that most of it went straight out to sea, untreated. A part of these improvements was the £8 million Pwllheli and Llanbedrog schemes, completed in 1999 at Gimlet Rock.

Co-operatives.
The corrugated iron building still stands of the Llŷn Co-operative Agricultural Society at Minafon, Llangwnnadl, looking none too different from the day it closed in 1928, having operated for only 15 years. It was the purchase of a steam traction engine for cartage to and from Pwllheli that did for it, at a time when steam traction was nearing it's end.

This was just one of the farmers co-operatives in Llŷn. Co-ops were much talked about at the beginning of last Century. In 1906 a group of young farmers met in Pencaenewydd, and formed Eifionydd Farmers Association two years later. This organisation served the farming community for 98 years before being taken over in 2004 by the Wynnstay Group, which itself began life as a farmers co-op.

The South Caernarfonshire Creamery (Hufenfa De Arfon) began life as a co-op in 1938, and is still a co-op today.

When the auction mart at Bryncir faced closure after the foot and mouth epidemic in 2001, it was taken over by a farmer based co-operative.

Following the BSE crisis in 1999, 40 beef producers founded the Llŷn Beef Producers Co-op. By 2003 it had 320 members.

Away from the agricultural sector, the first Co-operative Village Society, Antur Aelhaearn, in Britain was formed in 1974 at Llanaelhaearn. The factory it owns is used as a youth training centre, and it has plans to redevelop the disused Capel y Babell.

Up the hill in Llithfaen, in 1988 local people formed a co-op to run the successful pub Tafarn y Fic. And 10 years ago the shop,

Tafarn y Fic, Llithfaen – a co-operative village pub and Brenin Enlli, one of the local ales of Cwrw Llŷn brewery

Siop Pen y Groes, was purchased as a community business, and today runs as a non-profit making business by volunteers.

The Nefyn Town Trust began life to ensure the people of the town could drink clean water and have street lighting. Today it cares for the town's historic monuments and owns 26 houses which it lets to local people.

In C18th and C19th ship ownership on Llŷn was co-operative, each vessel being divided into 64ths, and shares purchased by individuals in the community. Mutual marine insurance companies followed (there were 5 in Nefyn alone) and Friendly Societies too, in which people would insure themselves against ill health and death.

Low Flying Jet Aircraft

Most of the low flying jets you'll see (and hear) are Hawk T Mk 4's from Valley RAF base on Anglesey. For the last fifty years this has been the training base for fast jet combat pilots, and you'll often see them performing noisy acrobatics. Foreign pilots from countries which ban low-flying aircraft are also trained in Llŷn's air space.

It is not unusual to see the yellow Sea King Search and Rescue helicopters too, especially towards the mountains.

Valley became a vital part of the allied support for Britain in the last World War, being the main receiving airport for flights from the USA, up to 60 or 70 planes a day.

There is no weekend flying and if you hear the planes you'll know the forecast is good.

Glaslyn Ospreys

Since 2004 the RSPB have run a visitor centre and observatory for the breeding ospreys at Glaslyn. It closes for the winter, as the birds head South to more pleasant climates.
See www.rspb.org.uk/community/blogs/glaslynospreys

Local Breweries

The local brew in the western peninsula is Cwrw Llŷn, a co-operative company set up in 2011 by twelve local entrepreneurs. Their flagship bitter is the clear and hoppy 'Brenin Enlli', on sale in local pubs. A golden ale, Seithenyn, also by Cwrw Llŷn, commemorates the legend of the drowned lands of Cantre'r Gwaelod in Bae Ceredigion. Their micro-brewery is at Nefyn, www.cwrwllyn.com and you can follow their latest news on twitter and facebook. Bragdy Mws Piws, the Purple Moose Brewery, is a 10 barrel micro-brewery in Porthmadog and began brewing in June 2005. There are four standard beers and plenty of other specials. The beers have won prizes and awards up and down the country. There is a brewery shop, and brewery tours. The beer is available in many pubs and shops in Llŷn. www.purplemoose.co.uk

Cycling further a field

Companion volumes are planned for both Ynys Môn (*Anglesey*) and Eryri (*Snowdonia*), but in the meantime, here is some information on cycling beyond Llŷn.

1 Lôn Las Cymru (Sustrans Route 8)

Lôn Las Cymru passes through Llŷn as it journeys from Holyhead to Cardiff or Chepstow, 250 miles of challenging cycling. The northern approach to Llŷn is via Lôn Las Menai, a 4 mile railway path from Y Felinheli to Caernarfon, and Lôn Eifion, the railway path through Llanwnda to Penygroes and Bryncir. To the south the route splits in Penrhyndeudraeth, with Route 8 going South via Barmouth, and Route 82 travelling through Trawsfynydd to Dolgellau.

2 Llwybr Mawddach (*Mawddach Trail*)

A railway path from Barmouth to Dolgellau, 15 km (9½ miles) in length.

3 Lôn Dysynni

From Tywyn along the Dysynni valley at the base of Cadair Idris.

4 Lôn Las Ogwen

11 miles of challenging cycling beginning on the railway path at Porth Penrhyn (Bangor) and rising to Llŷn Ogwen.

5 Bike Routes around Bala

www.visitbala.org. A series of rides in the district.

6 Coed y Brenin

One of the places to go for forest trail riding.

7 Other Websites

www.routes2bike.org.uk, for other bike routes in Wales.
www.cyclingnorthwales.co.uk. Rides, routes and a stack of other information from North Wales CTC.

Key to sketch maps

- ‑‑‑ Cycle path

- ····· Footpath

- ◯ Roundabout

- P Parking

- 🍺 Pub or Hotel

- S Shop

- ☕ Cafe

- + Church or Chapel

- π Cromlech

- Ⅹ Camping/Caravans

1 Lôn Eifion

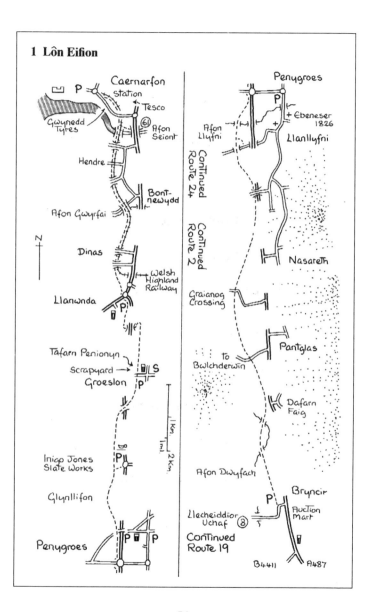

Caernarfon
Station
P
Tesco
Gwynedd Tyres
61
Afon Seiont
Hendre
Bont-newydd
Afon Gwyrfai
N
Dinas
Welsh Highland Railway
Llanwnda
P
Tafarn Penionyn
Scrapyard →
S
Groeslon
P
Inigo Jones Slate Works
P
1 Km
1 mi
2 Km
Glynllifon
Penygroes
P P

Penygroes
P
+ Ebeneser 1826
Afon Llyfni
+
Llanllyfni
Continued Route 24
Continued Route 2
Nasareth
Graianog Crossing
Pantglas
To Bwlchderwin
Dafarn Faig
Afon Dwyfach
Bryncir
P
Llecheiddior Uchaf 8
Auction Mart
Continued Route 19
B4411
A487

54

Lôn Eifion

Distance *20km (12.5mls) each way*

Grade *Popular (Easy, in comparison) and Family*

Many cyclists ride this cycle path one way and then the other, but take it wherever you come upon it, you can bowl along quite merrily. It also makes a perfect Family ride.

Lôn Eifion is a linear path from Caernarfon to Bryncir. It has gentle gradients and is tarmac'd the whole way (wide enough in places for a peloton), though several dismounts are required to negotiate sets of double gates at road crossings. It is well used by cyclists and also by dog walkers and the two, not being natural bedfellows, rub along in a respectful, curmudgeonly sort of way. It is wholeheartedly recommended that silent cyclists give pedestrians adequate warming of their approach by engaging in mild banter, whistling, clearing of throat etc. I prefer this to an impersonal dong on the bell as it provides further opportunity for brief discourse/ expressions of thanks etc thereby encouraging rider/ dog owner detente.

The cycle path is accompanied by the main road for some of it's length, but not in an unduly intrusive way, and otherwise it is an entirely rural, traffic-free, hassle-free route with a wide variety of habitat to enjoy. Furthermore it takes you from Caernarfon castle to the edge of the mountains, including a tantalising vista through the Nantlle valley towards Yr Wyddfa (*Snowdon*). It is, in short, a gorgeous run with such variety that a return journey along the same piece of tarmac is no hardship at all.

Parking There are car parks in Caernarfon, Llanwnda, Groeslon, at the Inigo Jones Slate Works, Penygroes and Bryncir.

Refreshments Caernarfon obviously, and a cafe at the Inigo Jones Slate Works (with, among other things, some 'Tom Jones' knickers), plus pubs at Llanwnda (Goat Hotel), Groeslon (Tafarn Penionyn), Penygroes (Yr Afr – The Goat), Llanllyfni (Quarryman's Arms) and a mile beyond Bryncir on the A487 at Glandwyfach (The Goat Inn). A little way beyond this is the Madhia Tandoori Restaurant at Garndolbenmaen. Why so many goats? It was the heraldic emblem of Snowdonia and old Caernarfonshire.

At the Aviation Museum in Pant Glas there has been an al fresco cafe, but at the time of writing there is some doubt about it's future.

Lôn Eifion

When the LMS railway line from Caernarfon to Afon Wen closed in 1964, the track bed to Bryncir was purchased by the local authority, and reopened as a footpath and cycle track in the 1980's. It forms part of Sustrans Route 8 Lôn Las Cymru, the Welsh National cycle route. In 1997 the cycle path was shifted over to accommodate the newly restored Welsh Highland Railway which accompanies the path from Caernarfon to Dinas. Also running alongside, but barely visible, is the Nantlle tramway, on which horse drawn trams carried slate from Nantlle to the harbour at Caernarfon.

Dinas station has been restored to it's 1923 appearance, and is surrounded by the sheds and works of the railway company, hence the redolent rusting hulks.

The Wall

The cycle path is accompanied for a couple of miles by the Wall. This is a boundary wall for the Glynllifon estate, 3m. (10ft) high, and 12km (8miles) long, it is still complete, and is itself a Grade 2 Listed Building.

The beginning of Lôn Eifion in Caernarfon

2 Clynnog

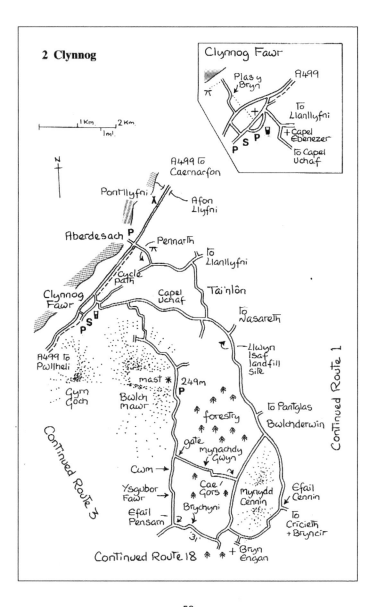

Clynnog Fawr

Plas y Bryn

A499

To Llanllyfni

Capel Ebenezer

To Capel Uchaf

P S P

1 Km. 2 Km.

1 ml.

N

A499 To Caernarfon

Pont Llyfni

Afon Llyfni

Aberdesach P

Pennarth

To Llanllyfni

Cycle Path

Capel Uchaf

Tai'nlôn

Clynnog Fawr

P S

To Nasareth

A499 To Pwllheli

Llwyn Isaf landfill site

Gyrn Goch

mast

249m

P

Bwlch mawr

forestry

To Pantglas

Bwlchderwin

gate

Mynachdy Gwyn

Cwm

Ysgubor Fawr

Cae'r Gors

Mynydd Cennin

Efail Cennin

Brychyni

To Criccieth + Bryncir

Efail Pensarn

Continued Route 3

Continued Route 1

Continued Route 18

Bryn Engan

58

Clynnog

Distance *22km (14 mls)*

Grade *Popular (Medium)*

*For a longer run combine with either Route 3 Yr Eifl,
or Route 1 Lôn Eifion.*

The big, bald hills are Gyrn Ddu, Gyrn Goch and Bwlch Mawr, and
they oversee this coastal strip like customs officers at Holyhead.
Nobody much hangs about here, they can't wait to partake of the
temptations beyond, and to reinforce this view, the eyes of the
Council surveyed the soaring peaks and sandy beaches of Llŷn
and thought, where do we put the Tip (otherwise known as the
Landfill site), and here it is. I like it here, it's peaceful and relaxed,
the only vehicle you're likely to meet is the Nicholas Cage-look-
alike postman, and this run is lovely, blossoming slowly into a full
panorama of firstly the mountains of Eryri (Snowdonia) and then
of Ynys Môn (Anglesey).

Parking On the coast at Aberdesach or Clynnog Fawr. There is
room for a couple of cars by the mast under Bwlch Mawr.

Camping/Caravans Also on the coast, at Pontllyfni.

Refreshments The pub, Y Beuno, is in Clynnog Fawr, so is the shop.

The coast is not the main attraction here. It is a low lying, shingly beach.

The Run

I heartily recommend doing this run clockwise. There's a fair bit of climbing, but you don't want to start up the steep hill onto Bwlch Mawr. From Aberdesach, cross the main road and take the minor road marked *Anaddas i Gerbydau Llydan* (Unsuitable for wide vehicles), a candidate for understatement of the year. The ride is hilly, for a while you hold your breath passing the landfill site, then you're on a boggy plateau around 160 m (500 ft) high, and here you'll find bilberries, blackberries, heather, harebells, and in the air screeching jays and a variety of raptors. Near Bwlchderwin a farm specialises in rare breeds. For much of the way up here there is just the sound of the wind in the trees and tinkling mountain streams.

Choose your road, either side of Mynydd Cennin, and at Efail Pensarn take a left and begin the steady, gentle climb to the mast, along a narrow back road with hardly enough room to fit a bike past a vehicle. From the mast the high mountain beyond the Arfon TV Transmitter is Yr Wyddfa (*Snowdon*). The road now plunges from 249 m (800 ft) down to sea level. Stretched out before you is Bae Caernarfon, the entrance to the Menai Strait and the South-western coast of Ynys Môn.

Burial Chambers

Throughout Clynnog are the slight remains of ancient occupation. At Pennarth is a Bronze Age burial chamber, a cromlech. Off the beaten track, near Clynnog Fawr is a Neolithic (C4th/early C3rd BC) burial chamber. The capstone has 110 cup-marks and 2 shallow grooves carved into it. What does it all mean? To find it, take the footpath across the main road from the church towards the sea. As the lane turns right to Bachwen, access to the coast is straight ahead, and to the left is the cromlech. Follow the track/footpath for a kilometre (0.5 Mile).

St Beuno's Church, Clynnog Fawr
The present substantial church is C16th, but it was founded 700 years before that, and became a gathering place for pilgrims to Ynys Enlli. Look for;-
• the ancient stone sundial,
• St Beuno's Chest. Medieval. Even the padlocks are 400 years old.
• Dog tongs, for removing annoying dogs from the church.

Chapels By the end of C18th many people in this parish were worshipping in Nonconformist chapels. Capel Uchaf (1750) was the first Calvinistic chapel, followed by Capel Brynaerau (1761), near Pontllyfni; then Bwlchderwin (1819); Seion in Gyrn Goch (1826); Ebeneser (1843) and Pant Glas (1868). The Baptists built Siloh chapel in Pontllyfni in 1812.

Burial chamber at Pennarth, Clynnog Fawr

3 Around Yr Eifl

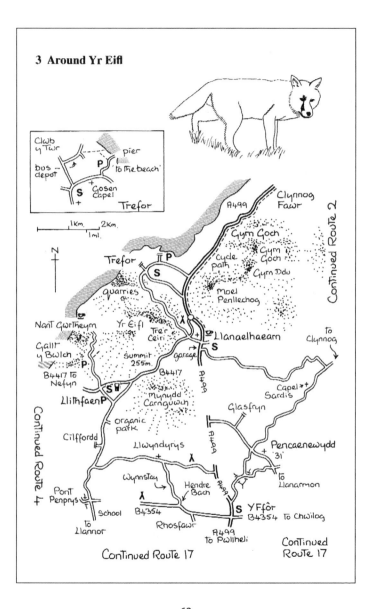

Clwb y Twr
bus depot
P
pier
'to the beach'
Gosen Capel
S
Trefor

1Km. 2Km.
1ml.
N

A499
Clynnog Fawr
Trefor
P
S
Cym Coch
cycle path
Cym Coch
Cym Ddu
quarries
Moel Penllechog
Nant Gwrtheyrn
Yr Eifl
Tre'r Ceiri
Llanaelhaearn
S
Gallt y Bwlch
P
Summit 255m.
garage
To Clynnog
B4417 To Nefyn
B4417
A499
Capel Sardis
S
Llithfaen P
Mynydd Carnguwch
Glasfryn
organic park
A499
Cilffordd
Llwyndyrys
Pencaenewydd '31'
Wynnstay
Hendre Bach
A499
To Llanarmon
Pont Penprys
School
To Llannor
B4354
Rhosfawr
S
Y Ffôr
B4354 To Chwilog
A499 To Pwllheli

Continued Route 2
Continued Route 4
Continued Route 17
Continued Route 17

Around Yr Eifl

Distance *30 km (19 mls)*

Grade *Popular (Medium)*

For a longer ride, link this with Route 2 Clynnog.

You would never say that this is the most attractive of rides, but this may have something to do with the ability of Yr Eifl to generate cloud, be it cloying mist or cloud driven against the mountain off the sea. It's a dramatic ride, passing through parts of Llŷn rarely explored. For a part of this ride you are in the hills, and the easier ascents are encountered if you travel clockwise.

Parking By the pier in Trefor, and in or above the village of Llithfaen. There are lay-by's too on the road between the two.

Caravans/Camping There are a couple of sites in the vicinity of Y Ffôr.

Refreshments The pub in Llanaelhaearn is now a cafe. The Tafarn y Fic in Llithfaen has a good reputation. There is a cafe too down in Nant Gwrtheyrn.

The Coast Access at Trefor and Nant Gwrtheyrn. The triple summits of Yr Eifl (564 m-1863 ft) provide as potent a symbol of

Llŷn as you would wish, plunging cliffs, old workings, shapely hills crowned with history.

The Run (from Trefor). Cycle up to the main road (A499), cross, and follow the cycle path south around the roundabout towards Llanaelhaearn. Unfortunately the path disappears for the last half a kilometre into the village. Remember to cycle positively in the main road, not in the gutter, make cars and lorries overtake you and not squeeze by. It's up a hill so you won't be travelling quickly. At the end of the village, almost opposite the garage, turn left onto an unsigned minor road. This is a quiet, flattish run through pasture and woodland. Capel Sardis sits on its own. Cycle across the next cross roads, this is Pencaenewydd, though you'd hardly know it, and down back to the main road. On your right is the Four Crosses sub-station, the electrical heartbeat of Llŷn. Into Y Ffôr and turn right at Ysgoldy M C, the Methodist chapel schoolroom. One kilometre on the B4354 through Rhosfawr, and it's a right turn at Hendre Bach wood yard. From here it's a gentle climb back up to Llithfaen, through a woody, scrubby, mossy, boggy part of Llŷn. Spot the three butterflies, a rare surviving example of a once ubiquitous species.

The car park above Llithfaen is up a steep hill from the centre of the village, and a visit to the Language Centre at Nant Gwrtheyrn, and cafe involves a long drop down to the shore. Otherwise, bypass the village and it's a short climb up to the summit on the B4417 below Yr Eifl, and then a long descent back to Llanaelhaearn. Close to the church take the narrow road to the left, directing you to a pottery, this is a tiny switchback road with fantastic views down the coast, and a final steep plunge down into Trefor.

Trefor

Samuel Holland, quarry owner, opened the quarry in 1850, and renamed the village (formerly Yr Hendre) after his foreman Trefor Jones. The pier was built in 1870 and a railway connection made to the bottom of the incline, said to be the steepest incline of any granite quarry in Britain. The big derelict crusher was built in 1923. The pier is closed (but used illegally by fishermen and divers) and is threatened with demolition. Apparently, the 'high crushing strength' of the granite makes it irresistible to curlers. The Canada Curling Stone Co. in Komoka, Ontario boasts exclusive rights on Trefor stones, which can be shades of blue, grey, red or brown, but most finished curling stones are composite Trefor/Ailsa Craig. Their low water absorption rate gives them a life of 40/50 years. The quarry employs 5. In it's heyday 700 used to work here.

Llanaelhaearn

In the churchyard are early Christian inscribed stones, dating from C5th/C6th.

Y Ffôr (Four Crosses)

Originally known as Uwchgwystl, the name Y Ffôr is from the Fourcrosses Inn, built in the early C19th at the intersection of two turnpike roads. Housing and two chapels, Ebenezer (Calvinist) and Salem (Independent) followed.

The main employer is the South Caernarfonshire Creamery (Hufenfa De Arfon), begun as a farmer's co-operative in 1938 and still a co-op today with 150 farmer members. As well as Dragon brand milk, over 10,500 tonnes of cheese is made each year (Old Shire, Dragon Cheddar, Caws Llŷn range and Monteray Jack).

Glasfryn Park

Activity and adventure centre; karting, bowling, wakeboarding, etc, and the track is used by the local cycling club.

Yr Eifl (The Rivals)

These mountains were misinterpreted by a visiting Englishman as 'the Rivals' many years ago – the Welsh name actually means 'a pair of forks', as the two passes between the peaks resemble upside-down open legs! Tre'r Ceiri means 'Town of the Giants'. On the summit are the remains of the outer wall and gateway, and 150+ round huts belonging to 'one of the finest examples' of an Iron Age hill fort.

Nant Gwrtheyn (and the Caffi Meinir)

Restored in 1978 as a National Language Centre.
Nant Gwrtheyn translates as Vortigern's Valley. Traditionally this was the last refuge of the Britonic High King Vortigern who came here in AD 450 to escape his Saxon enemies, Hors and Hengist.

Porth y Nant was a quarry village with 24 houses, a shop and a chapel, built in 1863 for workers in the 3 nearby quarries. Everything came and went by ship using 3 wooden jetties. The quarries closed in the 1930's, the last resident left in 1959.

Yr Eifl across the bay from Dinas Dinlle

The Mountains of Nefyn

Distance *Shorter Run 19 km (12 mls)*
Longer Run 24 km (15 mls)

Grade *Popular (Medium)*

***For longer runs combine with any of the neighbouring
routes.***

This is a run of two halves. For maximum drama, begin down on
the coast in Nefyn or Morfa Nefyn, and slowly work around anti-
clockwise, to the South side of the mountains, Garn Boduan,
Mynydd Nefyn and Gwylwyr, the soft side, ending up on the high
moor land road at a cruising height of 200 m (650 ft), before
plunging down into Pistyll and again to Nefyn.

Parking Nefyn, the big car park.
Morfa Nefyn, the National Trust car park.
Also at Pistyll, and there's room for a few cars at the foot of Garn
Boduan, plus near the AA box at Plas Boduan.

Caravans/Camping Choice of sites along the coast.

Refreshments Cafes and pubs/hotels in Nefyn and Morfa Nefyn,
and also the inn, Y Bryncynan by the roundabout on the Pwllheli
road.

4 Mountains of Nefyn

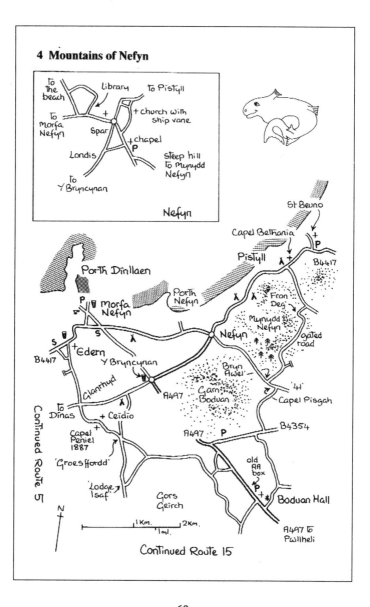

To the beach

library

To Pistyll

+ church with ship vane

To Morfa Nefyn

Spar

+ chapel

P

Londis

Steep hill To Mynydd Nefyn

To Y Bryncynan

Nefyn

St Beuno

Capel Bethania

P

Pistyll

B4417

Porth Dinllaen

Porth Nefyn

Fron Deg

Mynydd Nefyn

gated road

P

Morfa Nefyn

S

Nefyn

Edern

Y Bryncynan

Bryn Awel

B4417

Glanrhyd

Garn Boduan

'41'

Capel Pisgah

To Dinas

+ Ceidio

A497

Capel Peniel 1887

A497

P

B4354

'Groesffordd'

old AA box

'Lodge Isaf'

Gors Geirch

P

Boduan Hall

N

1 Km.   2 Km.
1 ml.

A497 to Pwllheli

Continued Route 5

Continued Route 15

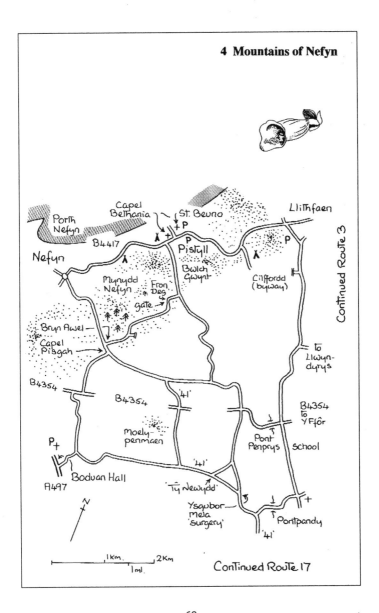

The Coast Access to the two huge bays at Morfa Nefyn and Nefyn. This is a dramatic piece of coastline, from the low lying headland at Porth Dinllaen round the bays to the steep headlands of Penrhyn Bodeilas and Penrhyn Glas. The mountains add to the drama. These are Garn Boduan (279 m – 911 ft), Mynydd Nefyn (228 m), Carreglefain (261 m), and Gwylwyr (237 m).

The Run

It is not at all difficult to take a wrong turning here, so let me talk you through it.

From Morfa Nefyn drop into Edern, turn left at Y Llong (*The Ship*) and head for Glanrhyd, a wartime camp converted to holiday places. Cross the Dinas road and pass Ceidio church on your left (medieval, ruined) and Peniel chapel on your right. At the crossroads near the house 'Groesffordd' (*groes* is Cross; *ffordd* is roads) meet those who have travelled here direct from Nefyn via Y Bryncynan roundabout. Pick your way along minor, unsignposted roads to Boduan. On your right is Gors Geirch, a National Nature Reserve (see Gors Geirch Circular Route 15). On your left is Garn Boduan, one of the line of volcanic hills which form the backbone of Llŷn. On the summit is an Iron Age hill fort with the remains of curtain walls and 170 roundhouses.

Cross the A497. Plas Boduan was a family home of the Wynne's, and through marriage in C18th, it passed into the hands of Lord Newborough of Glynllifon. The present Hall dates from around 1500 and hosted Ann Boleyn in her youth. It changed hands recently for a couple of million pounds. The sad-looking church was erected in 1765 and restored in 1840.

The recommended shorter route is to take an immediate left at Plas Boduan up the small wooded valley lined with rhododendron, cross the B4354, climbing gently all the while, to the small settlement of Penygarnedd (not that there's any sign).

Cross the old Nefyn road onto the flanks of Mynydd Nefyn. The panorama from this road is fantastic, from Yr Eifl right down the coast of Wales to the Mynyddoedd Preseli in Pembrokeshire. Finish the ride by dropping through Bwlch Gwynt (*bwlch*: pass; *gwynt*: wild)) and down to Pistyll. A short detour will take you to Eglwys St Beuno. Back to Capel Bethania and it's downhill most of the way to Nefyn.

For the longer, flatter run, take the right turn after Plas Boduan and wander the quiet, leafy lanes, crossing the stream which eventually tumbles to the sea below Pistyll, passing through tiny settlements before joining the main route at Pistyll.

Church of St Beuno, Pistyll
The church dates from C12th, with a Celtic font and the roof was thatched until 150 years ago. It is often decorated with medicinal herbs and other plants, with rushes strewn on the floor. During restoration in 1949 the remains of a C14th mural were found on plaster made of lime and beef fat. Of the three windows, one was specifically for the use of lepers.

On nearby Cefnydd Hill there used to be a hospice, inn and a monastery for the benefit of pilgrims.

Plas Pistyll
Now semi-derelict, this house was built for Mr Goddard of Leicester, the maker of polish for silver, which is still available today.

Capel Bethania, Pistyll
On the wall is a plaque with a portrait of Tom Nefyn Williams, quarryman, benefactor and evangelist, a charismatic speaker by all accounts.

Penrhyn Bodeilas

In 1839 the brig *Sappho* went down, with all hands lost except an apprentice found floating in a treacle barrel. They are buried in the churchyard in Nefyn.

Quarrying

On the beach close by the existing caravan parks are the remains of a pier and old quarry buildings. Quarrying was an important local employer, though the work was long and hard. The four main quarries on the hillsides were; Gwaith John Lloyd and Foel Dywrch on Mynydd Nefyn, Gwylwyr Quarry on Mynyd Gwylwyr, Tŷ Mawr or Bodeilas Quarry at Penrhyn Bodeilas, and the Moel Tŷ Gwyn Quarries known as the Vaenol and the Nanhoron.

St Mary's, Nefyn

Grey seals, often seen on Carreg Llam beach

Nefyn bay

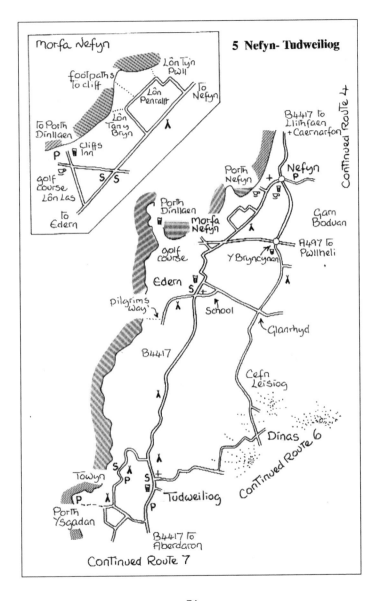

5 Nefyn- Tudweiliog

Morfa Nefyn

Lôn Tyn Pwll
footpaths to cliff
Lôn Penrallt
To Nefyn
Lôn Tan y Bryn
To Porth Dinllaen
Cliffs Inn
P
golf course
Lôn Las
S   S
To Edern

B4417 To Llithfaen + Caernarfon

Continued Route 4

Porth Nefyn

Nefyn
P

Garn Boduan

Porth Dinllaen

Morfa Nefyn

golf course

A497 To Pwllheli

Y Bryncynan

Edern
S

'Pilgrims Way'

School

Glanrhyd

B4417

Cefn Leisiog

Dinas

Continued Route 6

Towyn
S
P
S

Tudweiliog
P

Porth Ysgadan
P

B4417 To Aberdaron

Continued Route 7

74

Nefyn – Tudweiliog

Distance The circuit 20 km (12.5 miles)

Grade Easy (in comparison) The Family Run Edern –
Tudweiliog – Dinas – Edern 11 km (7 miles)

**For longer runs, this fits in beautifully with Route 6 Garn
Fadryn and Route 7 North Coast Explorer.**

The Run.

For much of the year not much happens here; the happy and free
hens lay eggs, the two Gareths fix cars and serve petrol, dogs are
walked, John ac Alun play guitar, the wind blows. In November
the car rally comes through at 3 on a cold, frosty Sunday morning.
Then in July for a couple of months, caravans arrive, tents are
erected, the sun shines, patience is exercised ("Two tins of beans
"-two raised fingers, pointing, spoken in loud, slow English),
wetsuits are dusted off and families are parked here while Dad
commutes back to Manchester. And livings are made.

This is a nice run. Unfortunately you're not running along the
coast, so you'll need to pop down there now and then to check
out the shore. It's fairly easy cycling, except that you cannot avoid
the B4417 on which you'll encounter some cars. Admittedly, not
many, but by the standards of Llŷn, there are vehicles. Plus there
are a couple of hills, in and out of Edern, in and out of Tudweiliog,
though only 20/30 m (60/90 ft) each. You climb up to Dinas too,

that's 30/40 m (90/ 125 ft). Otherwise it's flat. Porth Ysgadan is accessed down a rough track, but it's well worth it.

A hundred years ago it was different, totally different. Nowadays much of the money spent in Llŷn, leaves Llŷn. It goes to the mega-rich Walton family in the USA (via Asda); Dieter Schwarz (via Lidl); Peter Harf (A B Inbev); Povl Krogsgaard-Larson (Carlsberg); Rex W. Tillerson of Texas (ExxonMobil); the Porsche family and the Emirate of Qatar (VW); the Mars family; Peter Brabeck-Letmothe (Nestle); and China (anything else). Before globalisation the money made in Llŷn, stayed in Llŷn, and this little patch illustrates this perfectly.

Parking In Nefyn, Morfa Nefyn, Tudweiliog, Porth Ysgadan, and there's room for a couple of cars near the school in Edern in the hols.

Camping/Caravans There are a couple of sites around Nefyn, and around Tudweiliog, plus Hirdre Fawr, half way between.

Refreshments
Cafe's – In Nefyn, behind the Post Office, near the roundabout, and down towards Porth Nefyn. In Morfa Nefyn, opposite the NT car park. Also there's a caravan site shop at Towyn.
Pubs – There are more pubs on this page than anywhere else in this book.
Nefyn, Nanhoron Arms, Y Folt wine bar, Sportsman Inn,
Y Bryncynan, out of town.
Morfa Nefyn, Cliffs Inn.
Porthdinllaen, Ty Coch Inn (see later).
Edern, Y Llong.
Tudweiliog, Lion Hotel.

The Coast It's a low, rocky shoreline topped with clay, with several coves and beaches. The coastal footpath follows the shore, but access to the middle bit is limited. Near Tudweiliog, the Porth Towyn beach is popular, and Porth Ysgadan beach is unusual. The large beaches at Porth Nefyn and Porth Dinllaen are mixed pebbles and sand (which comes and goes as the winter winds move around the sea currents) and provide shelter for small boats. The beach at Porth Dinllaen, with the Tŷ Coch Inn right there on the beach, is deservedly popular, and the walk from there past the lifeboat station can sometimes be rewarded by the sight of basking seals at Carreg Ddu.

Nefyn and Morfa Nefyn.
Let us start in the centre of Nefyn, near the crossroads behind the public toilets. Climb the watchtower, built in 1846 to espy the herring fleet, and built on the mutilated ruins of a medieval castle., and look across to St Mary's church (converted to a museum, which volunteers are hoping to reopen). The church was rebuilt in 1827, adjoining an ancient Celtic religious house. The weather vane is a sailing ship. The town's insignia is Three Herrings. Beyond the weather vane, on the mountain sides are the quarries. These produced setts, used to pave the streets of English industrial towns, and superseding the paving or cobble stones, which were also exported from Nefyn and Morfa Nefyn to Liverpool, for onward passage by canal. In the other direction you'll have to imagine the tall chimney stack of the brickworks, where the National Trust car park is now in Morfa Nefyn.

If you cycle on the back road between Nefyn and Morfa Nefyn you can gain access to the cliff top above the beaches, and then on to Morfa Nefyn, where you now see holidaymakers, a jet ski perhaps, or beach fisherman, these beaches were once Llŷn's gateway to the outside world.

For 400 years local men have sailed their own boats from Llŷn to Liverpool and Chester. Out went herring, corn, butter, cheese, hens and especially pigs. In came hops, pepper, wood, cloth, clay pipes, salt, iron, vinegar, sugar, soap. In the C18th seaweed and bracken were burned to produce ashes for soap making in Liverpool, Warrington and Chester (read Jim Crace's excellent book 'Signals of Distress').

Gradually ships went further afield, Dublin, Belfast, Cork, Waterford; Bristol and Gloucester; Workington and Whitehaven; and on to Exeter, Bridport, London, Newcastle and Glasgow. Oak came from Conwy, pine from the Baltic and Canada. Limestone was imported to burn in local kilns for house mortar and fertiliser, and coal from Lancashire, the northern coast of Wales and Swansea. At Bwlch, down from the Cliffs Inn, an offshore wooden platform was built and coal unloaded into buckets and brought ashore on an aerial system of wires and pulleys.

In the year 1840, 914 ships put in to Nefyn and Porth Dinllaen. The two bays were alive with fishing boats, especially herring boats. It was a part time business, from late summer to early winter, using drift nets. By 1800 there were 40 boats in the bay at Nefyn, with ancillary storehouses and curing sheds. Most were exported, either salted (white herring) or smoked (red herring).

The bays were also alive with ship building. Many small one-masted boats were built here, and in the C18th these were mostly sailing sloops of 14 to 30 tons. In 1784 the *Prince of Orange*, a 78 ton brigantine was built in Nefyn Bay, and in 1788 *Peggy*, a 50 ton sloop. By the 1830's the boats were bigger; schooners for example, the *Cevn Amwlch* (1838 – 110 tons), *Superior* (1839 – 121 tons), the *Jane and Ellen* (1839 – 111 tons), and the *Vron* (1839 – 101 tons). Twenty years later the barques *Robert Thomas* (1855 – 335 tons) and *Isolina* (1866 – 390 tons) were constructed at Porth Nefyn, and the last to leave the stocks was the *Venus* in 1880 (107 tons).

All the ancillary trades were here too, ropewalks, sail lofts, sawpits, nailers, blacksmiths etc, and seafaring became a tradition, a hazardous tradition. Although two thirds of the boats built at Nefyn sailed for twenty years or more, eventually 72% were lost at sea.

Remains can be seen today along the shoreline, rust-encrusted rings in the rocks, the remnants of old slipways and ancient half-buried anchors.

At the end of Morfa Nefyn beach, towards Porth Dinllaen, the house on stilts was once a warehouse known as Warws Dora. *Dora* was a 300 – ton vessel, one of the steamships operated by the Aberdovey and Barmouth Steamship Co., which carried passengers and cargo between Liverpool, Porthdinllaen and Barmouth. David Williams of Morfa Nefyn was captain from 1909 until 1917 when the ship encountered a German submarine. Everyone was ordered into the lifeboats, and *Dora* was torpedoed.

Early in the C20th omnibuses served Nefyn from the railway station in Pwllheli and visitors arrived in numbers. From the 1930's onwards, some of the townspeople built chalets or sited caravans in their gardens and let out their houses to English visitors. This tradition continues today, though affected recently by the Authorities demanding increased payment of Council Tax. The peak time for visitors was the 1950's to the 1970's, when the beaches were packed, before the eyes of holidaymakers turned to Spain.

Porth Dinllaen
A popular holiday spot centred on the Tŷ Coch, the beach and the boats. One of the cottages here has a display which tells you all you need to know. It is perhaps fortunate that Porth Dinllaen failed to become the main ferry terminal to Ireland. Up above is the golf course with the remains of ramparts and ditches from the C1st BC fort. Towards the headland, the lifeboat station was built in 1864, and the coastguard lookout is manned, once again, by volunteers.

Tŷ Coch and Porth Dinllaen

Porth Nefyn, with the Eifl across the bay

Nefyn: The Early Days.

Primitive Mesolithic nomadic hunter-gatherers reached Llŷn perhaps 10,000 years ago, followed by Neolithic farmers. In the Iron Age Celtic-speaking people came from central Europe and from Ireland (800 BC-100AD). The Romans largely ignored Llŷn, but from the late C4th the Irish came across the sea, Saxons moved in from England and Vikings down the coast. The Celtic Saints arrived in numbers too. The Normans were at first resisted by the Welsh Prince Gruffudd ap Cynan, but in 1282 the death of Llywelyn ap Gruffudd in battle and the execution of his brother Dafydd six months later meant that the power of the Princes of Gwynedd was finally destroyed and this very Welsh part of the world fell into the hands of the King of England.

In the summer of 1284 King Edward 1st (the builder of the grand castles at Caernarfon, Beaumaris, Conwy and Harlech) chose Nefyn as the venue for an elaborate celebratory tournament. In the fields towards the sea from the town, now called Cae Iorwerth (*Edward's field*) and Cae Ymryson (*the field of the contest*), an expensive and glamorous show was meant to impress. The town grew, the Black Prince granted a Royal Charter in 1355, confirming a weekly market and two annual fairs. Then the Black Death decimated the population, and in 1400 the followers of Owain Glyndŵr, revolted against foreign occupation and attacked and burnt imperial colonial towns in Wales. Nefyn was burned to the ground during those long years of confrontation.

Abergeirch bay

Access to the coast can be achieved from Lôn Cae Glan in Edern. The cove at Bryn Gwydd is one of those tiny, pebbly coves perfect for an afternoon snooze and a paddle. To the north-east is Abergeirch, the remnants of a building, and at low tide the cable itself, a reminder that this was the terminus for the telegraph to Ireland.

6 Garn Fadryn Circular

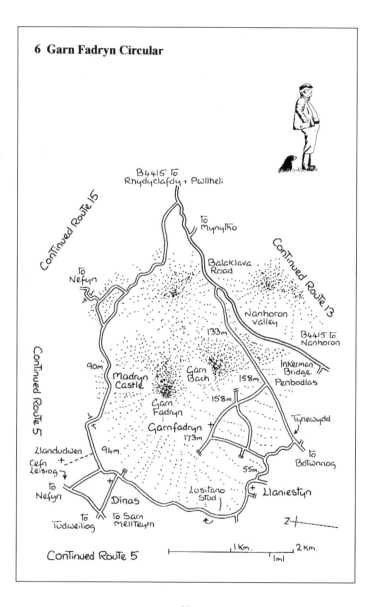

B4415 To
Rhydyclafdy + Pwllheli

To
Mynytho

Continued Route 15

Continued Route 13

Balaklava
Road

To
Nefyn

Nanhoron
Valley

133m

B4415 To
Nanhoron

90m

Madryn
Castle

Garn
Bach

158m

Inkerman
Bridge

Penbodlas

Continued Route 5

158m

Garn
Fadryn

Garnfadryn
173m

Tynewydd

Llandudwen

94m

To
Botwnnog

Cefn
Leisiog

55m

To
Nefyn

Dinas

Lusitano
Stud

Llaniestyn

To
Tudweiliog

To Sarn
Mellteyrn

Z

Continued Route 5

1 Km.   2 Km.
1 ml.

Garn Fadryn Circular

Distance *Round trip 15 km (9 mls) plus*
This route fits in beautifully with any of the neighbouring runs.

Grade Popular *(Medium)*

Garn Fadryn is the conical hill in the middle of Llŷn. You can't miss it. If you want to climb it (371 m/ 1200 ft), and you should, leave your bike or vehicle next to the chapel in the village of Garnfadryn and follow the well worn path. If you want to ride around it, and you should, this is what you do.

Whenever I think, where shall I go, this is where I come. It is a beautifully varied run with a bit of woodland, moor land, a valley, a few chapels, an old mill, pasture dropping away on all sides and ever changing views. Eryl, the postman, was a boy in the village of Garnfadryn, and before electricity arrived in 1958 he was told to be quiet every Saturday teatime as his father checked his Pools on the battery radio under the paraffin lamp on the piano. Mains water arrived at the same time, before that it was a half mile carry in a bucket from the stream.

Parking
Other than the small car park in the village of Garnfadryn there is no obvious place to park in the immediate vicinity, though you can find places to pull off the road a little. Better though to park in one of the surrounding villages and factor that into the loop.

Caravans/Camping

Clockwise from ten to ten; Llanbedrog, Mynytho, Neigwl, Bryncroes, Tudweiliog, Morfa Nefyn.

Refreshments

Nearest cafes are in Sarn Mellteyrn and Morfa Nefyn. Nearest pubs are in Rhydyclafdy (Tu Hwnt i'r Afon), Llanbedrog (Y Llong and Glyn y Weddw), Sarn (3), Tudweiliog (Lion), Edern (Ship) and Nefyn (Y Bryncynan).

The Run

Climbing: there's not much to choose between going one way around or the other, except, anti-clockwise, unless you want to really stretch yourself, don't do the loop up to the village of Garnfadryn, the climb up here is soul-destroying. There's a fair bit of up and down, and the highest points are; Madryn Castle (90m/ 300ft), near Penbodlas (133m/440ft), Garnfadryn (optional) (173m/ 600ft) and Dinas (94m/ 310ft).

Garn Fadryn

This conical hill is a monadnoch, a mountain of old, hard igneous rock (Ordovician granite) rising like an island out of a plateau. It can be spotted from most places in Llŷn. On the summit are the remains of a Bronze Age burial chamber, the C12th fort of Rhodri and Maelgwn, sons of Owain Gwynedd, but mostly what you notice, nestling in the heather, are the remains of 170 or so small stone huts, both inside and outside a defensive enclosure. It is thought they were lived in between 1,700 and 1,900 years ago (C2nd to C4th) when the Romans occupied most of eastern Britain and, elsewhere built bath-houses, and centrally heated villas with mosaic floors.

Llaniestyn

A scattered settlement centred around the Norman church of St Iestyn, and three chapels, and home, in 1998, of the oldest recorded duck, aged 25. It may still be alive!

Pen Llŷn Lusitano Stud and riding Centre. The UK's leading Lusitano Stud, featuring the magnificent white Portuguese stallion, Uivador da Broa. It offers hacks, trekking and lessons. See section on Meeting Horses.

Cefn Leisiog

Down the hill a bit from Dinas is Cefn Leisiog, now an innocent looking farm, but in the Second World War this was RAF Nevin, a Chain Home Radar Base, part of a coastal network designed to detect the Luftwaffe. There are remnants still of the bunkers and the supports for the elegant metal pylons.

Llandudwen Church

Also down the hill a little ways is this tiny church, mostly C12th with small, powerfully coloured stained glass windows, and illuminated inside by paraffin lamp. A mounting block is provided for the gentry, but most of the congregation walked. The first church was built here in C7th by an anchorite (not an early ancestor of Popeye, but an ascetic religious hermit called Tudwen). Across the fields, and now overgrown, is St Tudwen's well, the waters being useful to counter diseases of the eye, rheumatism and epilepsy.

Madryn

Among the caravans, one stone arch is all that remains of Madryn Castle. It was an agricultural college, and before that the ancestral seat of the Love Jones Parrys. Captain Love and Lewis Jones went to Patagonia in 1863, delivering, perhaps overenthusiastically, glowing reports on their return. The main group of 150 settlers followed on in the clipper *Mimosa* on 28 July 1865, and on arrival named the town Porth Madryn. Twinned with Nefyn, the Patagonian town and resort of Puerto Madryn has a population of 58,000, of whom several thousand still speak Welsh. Nefyn-raised Duffy stars in the 2011 film 'Patagonia'.

Balaklava Road

The B4415 Nanhoron to Rhydyclafdy road is known as the Balaklava Road. Down in the valley, near the Nanhoron Quarries, is Inkerman Bridge, which commemorates the death, on 5th November 1854 in the Crimean War of Captain Richard Lloyd Edwards aged 22. The valley of Afon Horon once contained a succession of water-powered fulling and corn mills, including the Saethon factory, 150 m to the South of Inkerman Bridge.

Porth Ysgadan

Schist and Gneiss at Porth Witlin

St Gwynhoedl church, Llangwnnadl

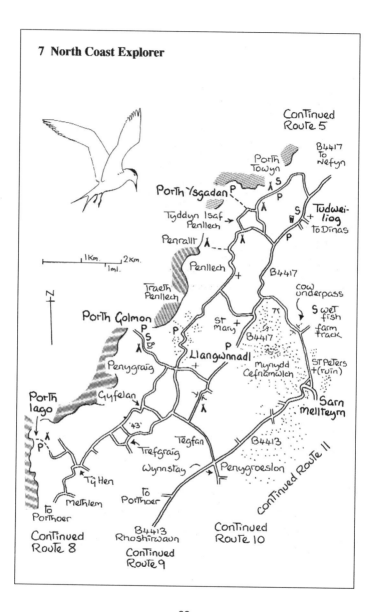

Continued
Route 5

B4417
To
Nefyn

Porth
Towyn

P S
P

Porth Ysgadan P

S
Tudwei-
liog
to Dinas
P

Tyddyn Isaf
Penllech

Penrallt

Penllech

B4417

1Km. 2Km.
1ml.

N

cow
underpass

Traeth
Penllech

St
Mary
B4417

S wet
fish
farm
track

Porth Golmon
P
S

P

Llangwnnadl

St Peters
+(ruin)

Penygraig

Mynydd
Cefnamwlch

Cufelan

Sarn
Mellteyrn

Porth
Iago
P

'43'

Tegfan

B4413

Continued Route 11

Trefgraig

Wynnstay

Penygroeslon

Ty Hen

To
Porthoer

Methlem

To
Porthoer

Continued
Route 8

B4413
Rhoshirwaun

Continued
Route 9

Continued
Route 10

North Coast Explorer

Tudweiliog – Porth Ysgadan – Porth Golmon
Porth Iago – Trefgraig Plas – Cefnamwlch

Distance *Family Run 12km (7mls)*
Popular Ride 24km (15mls)

Grade *Easy (in comparison)*

For a longer ride, link this run with Routes 8, 9 and 10.

A charming, flattish run exploring the coves and beaches of the northern shore, with plenty of choice. The northern coast of Llŷn is significantly different to the south. The water is colder. This is Bae Caernarfon, part of the Irish Sea, and not the lagoon of Bae Ceredigion. Sightings of dolphin and porpoise are rare, though seals are common enough. You need a calculator to work out the tides. The water rushes around the end and then slows when faced with a whole bay to fill. Currents are strong, as swimmers and boatmen alike can testify.

This section of coast doesn't have the melodrama of the South, there's none of the razzamatazz of Abersoch or the throng of Porthmadog. There's no sweep of coast for your eye to follow, no Cadair Idris, no Mynyddoedd Preseli to pick out as a smudge on the horizon. Instead there's Mynydd Twr (*Holyhead Mountain*), visible on most days, and often much of the rest of Ynys Môn too, sometimes on the horizon container ships heading for Liverpool glint in the sun, and to the left puffs of cloud give away the location of Ireland. The Wicklow Mountains are visible on a clear day, and every now and then you can pick out Shillelagh in County Wicklow and Mount Leinster and the Blackstairs Mountains in Wexford. Once or twice a year you get the Full Monty.

Parking
At, and near Tudweiliog, and various places along the coast, Traeth Penllech, Porth Golmon, Porth Iago. The field at Towyn Farm near Tudweiliog has an honesty box, so does Ty Mawr Farm at Porth Iago.

Caravans/Camping
Lots of choice right along the coast.

Refreshments
The shop is at Tudweiliog, so is The Lion. Camping sites at Porth Colmon and Towyn have shops/refreshments. Beyond Porth Iago, down the coast is the cafe at Porthoer.

The Run
I'm taking you along the coast, for occasional paddles and ice cream, returning on an inland run, with a choice of routes around the low, forested hill of Cefnamwlch.

The run from Tudweiliog to Porth Golmon is as pleasant a family run as you would wish (13k/8mls return). It rises at either end to Tudweiliog and to Penygraig. Porth Golmon to Porthoer is 12km/7mls return and pretty much flat. At Porthoer there are posts at the top of the hill to lock your bike to. The NT cafe and shop are down at the beach. You can also follow the bridleway down through the fields from the barn near Methlem (please remember to keep the gate shut).

The longer run, to Porth Iago and back around Cefnamwlch is 24k/ 15mls.

Tudweiliog

Most of the year a sleepy village, in summer the population rises significantly.

The church, St Cwyfan's, was entirely rebuilt in 1849 by George Gilbert Scott, specialist in workhouses, churches, the Albert Memorial and St Pancras Station.

Porth Ysgadan (The Herring Harbour)

As well as herring, this little harbour was an important link with the outside world, served regularly by small ships, with the goods transported inland by pony and cart. Coal and limestone were fired in the nearby lime kilns. The roofless building, used latterly as a store, was the home of the Customs Officer, and doubled up as a lighthouse.

Penllech

The Church, Eglwys Santes Fair (St Mary's) is small and ascetic. The building is Georgian. An earlier church housed one of the first schools around here. Henry Rowlands was first schooled here before going on to New College, Oxford, and then to become Bishop of Bangor in 1598. When he died he left money to found a local grammar school at Botwnnog, still the secondary school for this end of Llŷn.

Traeth Penllech

I've been told that the seaweed here is whisked away to the sushi bars of England.

Llangwnnadl

The church is old, founded in C6th by St Gwynhoedl, a stone building replaced the wooden one in Norman times, and further expansion took place in the Tudor period. Inside the gate a sundial has been placed on top of a medieval cross.

Porth Golmon

This was also a busy little harbour, employing it's own pilot. The last was Wil Llainfatw, with a face full of white whiskers. Cargoes were unloaded by hand, until the Llangwnnadl Co-operative mechanised the process. Using wood from a wreck, they built a shed which housed a steam engine, from which a wire rope ran down to the ship, onto which was attached a bucket which was winched ashore.

(www.rhiw.com contains some fascinating insights into the working of the harbour).

Porth Tŷ Mawr

A walk along the coast from Porth Golmon is Porth Tŷ Mawr, sometimes known as Porth Wisgi. At low tide the bones can be seen of S. S. Stewart, wrecked here a hundred years ago. It carried carpets and pottery, furniture and whisky.

Porth Iago

A striking beach, popular with anglers. There is a 50p charge for access by bicycle.

Mynydd Cefnamwlch

Set back from the road, but accessible, just beyond the cow underpass, is a Neolithic burial chamber, C4th or early C3rd BC. The legend is that the chambered tomb was once demolished by a farmer, and the stones carted away, but the grazing cows became disturbed and bellowed incessantly until the tomb was rebuilt.

A track leads off this road to Mary and Gareth at Selective Seafoods, for fresh crab, lobster, sea bass and mackerel, (www.se lectiveseafoods.com. The boatman, Siôn Williams, also does sight seeing and fishing trips.

Sunset over Bae Ceredigion

Mynydd Mawr and Ynys Enlli

8 The End

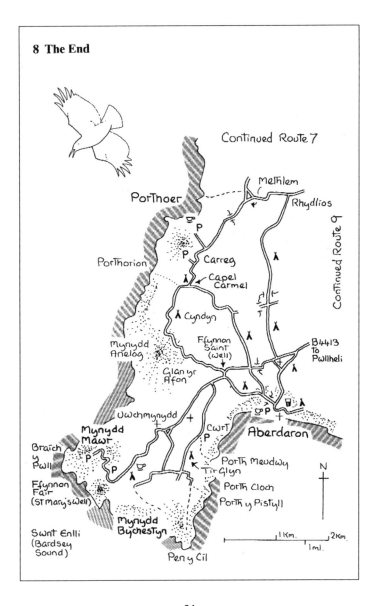

Continued Route 7

Methlem

Rhydlios

Porthoer

P

Porthorion

P

Carreg

Capel Carmel

Cyndyn

Ffynnon Saint (Well)

Mynydd Anelog

Glan yr Afon

Continued Route 9

B4413 To Pwllheli

Uwchmynydd

Mynydd Mawr

Braich y Pwll

Ffynnon Fair (St Mary's Well)

Swnt Enlli (Bardsey Sound)

P

P

Cwrt

P

Aberdaron

P

Porth Meudwy

Tir Glyn

Porth Cloch

Porth y Pistyll

Mynydd Bychestyn

Pen y Cil

N

1 Km.   2 Km.

1 ml.

94

The Far End

Aberdaron – Mynydd Mawr – Porthoer (*Whistling Sands*) – Aberdaron

Distance Popular run 22.5km (14mls)

Grade Easy/Medium
Family Run Aberdaron – Porthoer and return 10km (6mls)

For longer runs, combine with Routes 7 and 9 and beyond

The end of Llŷn is glorious. High above the steep cliffs plunging into the swirling waters of Swnt Enlli (*Bardsey Sound*), Mynydd Mawr commands a view which, on a clear day takes in the Wicklow Mountains, Ynys Enlli (*Bardsey*), Pembrokeshire, Cadair Idris, Yr Wyddfa (*Snowdon*) and Ynys Môn (*Anglesey*). The roads are narrow and hilly, though the climbs are short. Mostly the roads are quiet, although at the height of summer the cars of visitors head for Mynydd Mawr, and also Porthoer.

The route to and from Porthoer from Aberdaron is along quiet, undulating roads. The steepest section is out of Aberdaron.

Parking   Aberdaron (National Trust), Mynydd Mawr, Carreg, Porthoer (National Trust), Cwrt

Camping/Caravans Plenty of choice.

Refreshments

There are two cafe's in Aberdaron, and a cafe on the beach at Porthoer, and a cafe in a caravan site near Mynydd Mawr. Both pubs are in Aberdaron.

The Coast

Much of the coast is rocky cliff, with plenty of paths above. The beaches are in Aberdaron and Porthoer. Porth Meuddwy is a small cove. The ferry service to Ynys Enlli (*Bardsey*) leaves from here. The shore is also accessible at Ffynnon Fair (*St Mary's well*) and Porthorion.

Wildlife

Seals live in these waters, bottlenose dolphins too. Other coastal birds include tern and gannet, raven, fulmar, razorbill, kittiwake and guillemot. On the headland watch out for chough, wheatear, stonechat and meadow pipit

Aberdaron

A lovely village providing most of the basics, though it can heave with visitors in summer. The herons, Little Billy and Big Billy, fed by John the butcher, are engaged in constant warfare with the gulls. There used to be lots of local bakeries in Llŷn. Islyn Bakery, run by Alun Becws, is one of the last.

In the Middle Ages pilgrims rested and refuelled here on their way to Ynys Enlli (The tea room, Y Gegin Fawr – was established around 1300.) The church of St Hywyn and Saint Lleuddad dates from C12th, enlarged in C15th. It contains the Anelog Stones. These are the tombstones of two Christian priests, Veracius and Senacus, from the early C6th, found up the road on Anelog.

The old post office was designed by the prolific and fashionable Sir Bertram Clough Williams-Ellis, the architect of Portmeirion, the Battersea Dogs Home and the old Snowdon Cafe.

Aberdaron

The Gruffudd boys had fun here back in C11th. Gruffudd ap Cynan and his son in law Gruffudd ap Rhys made a habit of seeking sanctuary in the church, then slipping away to safety under cloak of night and returning to the battlefields to beat invading Norman armies. Happy days.

Richard Robert Jones ('Dic Aberdaron') was born in 1780 in a house on the way to Porthoer. He taught himself to read Welsh and English, and travelled widely from the age of 20. It was said that he could speak anything from 15 to 35 languages. He carried books in the pockets of his baggy, colourful, patched clothing, a French horn around his neck, and his travelling companion was a cat. He died at the age of 63 and is buried at St Asaph.

Glan yr Afon
Aberdaron Camp, for youth, used for over 40 years by the Seventh-Day Adventist Church.

Braich y Pwll
The headland is the only known location on the British mainland of the spotted rock rose, which produces bright yellow petals lasting only one day.

From the lower car park, walk towards the sea. The site is St Mary's chapel, also a medieval farm. Cultivation ridges are just visible. Ffynnon Fair can be found next to the sea down a few steps cut into the rock.

Carreg
The quarry at the base of the hill was an C18th and C19th Jasper mine. Carreg Plas was the home of Welsh chieftains. The present building dates from C16th.

Porthoer (*Whistling Sands*)

Take off your shoes, it really is more of a squeak.

Porthoer

9. Aberdaron Loops

B4413 To Rhoshirwaun

To Rhiw

bakery →

S

To Uwchmynydd

P

Aberdaron

To Llangwnnadl

Continued Route 7

Wynnstay

B4413 To Pwllheli

Penygroeslon

Rhydlios

B4413

Meillionydd

Methlem

Rhoshirwaun
Capel Saron

mynydd Rhiw

School

radar masts

Castell Odo

Felin Uchaf

Rhiw

Ffern Bodernabwy

new church

Trygfan

To Porth Neigwl

B4413 Pencaerau

St maelrhys

Aberdaron

Ysgo

P P

Nant y Gadwen

Continued Route 8

Continued Route 10

Porth Ysgo

Porth Cadlan

N

1 Km. 2 Km.
1 ml.

100

Aberdaron Loops

Distance Popular Run: Aberdaron – Rhiw – Penygroeslon – Rhydlios – Aberdaron. 17km (10½ miles)

Grade Easy (in comparison).
Family Run Aberdaron – Porth Ysgo – Rhoshirwaun – Aberdaron 10km (6mls)

For longer runs use any or all of the neighbouring Routes.

The Runs
These are as gentle as runs can be out of Aberdaron. Both climb out of the village, the Popular Run has extra climbing up to Rhiw. Probably the easier way around both runs is clockwise, but there's not much in it.

Parking Aberdaron, Porth Ysgo, Rhiw.

Caravans/Camping Lots around Aberdaron.

The Coast
At the end of Aberdaron beach is the headland Trwyn y Penrhyn, and beyond it the islands Ynys Gwylan Fawr and Ynys Gwylan Fach (*gwylan*: gull). These are both SSSIs and nesting sites for puffin, cormorant, razorbill and guillemot. Further around access to the shore is good at Porth Ysgo, and Porth Alwm. From the car park in Rhiw, paths take you onto the headland. This is all National Trust land.

Aberdaron

Aberdaron is one of the few British locations of a bright orange lichen called the golden hair lichen, an indication of exceptionally clean air.

The 'New' Church, at the top of the village, was completed in 1841 at a cost of £1,400 when it was feared the old church would be swept away by the sea. At the same time the ford below Bodernabwy Farm was replaced by the present bridge.

R. S. Thomas (1913-2000). Famous poet and Anglican clergyman, he was noted for his deep dislike of the Anglicisation of Wales, and critical of the Welsh too, for 'selling out'. He was curate of St Hywyn's and lived for a while in a bare cottage on the flanks of Rhiw. This poem was written on the death of his wife.

We met
under a shower
of bird-notes.
Fifty years passed
love's moment
in a world in
servitude to time.
She was young;
I kissed with my eyes
closed and opened
them to her wrinkles.
"Come," said death,
choosing her as his
partner for
the last dance, And she
who in life
had done everything
with a bird's grace,

opened her bill now
for the shedding
of one sigh no
heavier than a feather.

St Maelrhys

The lonely church of St Maelrhys is part medieval. The chapel at Pencaerau (now converted) was one of the earliest Nonconformist chapels, built in 1768.

Porth Ysgo and Porth Alwm

Access down the cliff on steps to the small beach and rocky shoreline. Adders are not unusual. You may spot young people with a crash mat below, 'bouldering', free climbing on the boulders. The rock is brilliant, apparently.

Around the coast is Porth Cadlan. A recent study has proposed the unremarkable valley above the porth as the site of the last battle fought by King Arthur in the C6th. Having been wounded by the forces of Medrawd (Mordred), Arthur was taken by boat from Porth Cadlan to Ynys Enlli where he was healed by the Elixir of Life, the Bardsey apple.

Manganese Mines (Rhiw/ Llanfaelrhys)

Manganese mining began here on a small scale in 1858, but it was during the two Wars, when supplies were unavailable from elsewhere, that production peaked. In the early days it was used to make bleach, glass, paint and varnish, but it's real utility was to toughen and harden steel in the smelting process, invaluable in the production of rails, ships, machinery, and armaments.

The two successful mines were in Nant Gadwen, in the valley above Porth Alwm, and high on Mynydd Rhiw below the radar mast at Benallt. 46,644 tons in total were extracted from Nant

Gadwen, but it shut in 1925 because of flooding. Benallt was reopened in 1938 and 60,000 tons extracted in 6 years, making it 195,000 in total. It shut for the last time in 1945. Although there were accidents, not one life was lost in these mines.

At first the ore was sent to the railway at Pwllheli, hauled by steam traction engine, but they mangled the roads. Small wooden sailing ships were also beached at Porth Cadlan and the ore transported to them by mule.

In 1902 a pier was built at Porth Ysgo at a cost of £182, and another pier at Porth Neigwl. To the latter the ore was carried over the village of Rhiw in 6 cwt buckets by aerial cable on pylons. From Benallt the mine wagons themselves were lowered down the hillside by cable drum, pulled to the cliff top first by horses them steam engine, and lowered down the two inclines to the pier.

Bits of the system can still be seen.

Felin Uchaf

Castell Odo

On the summit are the badly eroded ramparts of an early hill fort (late C2nd – C1st AD), and a pillow mound, probably C17th or C18th, an artificial rabbit-warren, an early form of rabbit farming.

Felin Uchaf

Holistic education centre providing training and courses in rural skills, eco-building, sustainable agriculture and Community Arts.

Porth Ysgo

Mynydd Mawr

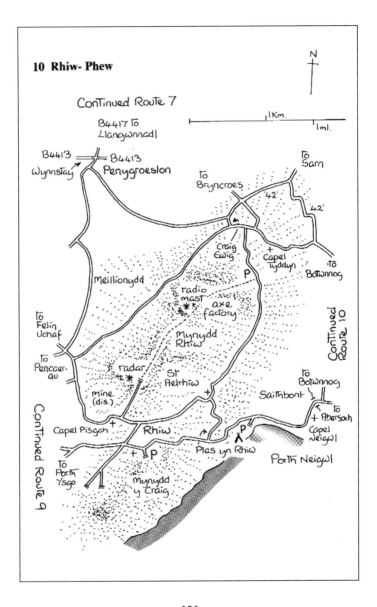

Continued Route 7

B4417 To Llangwnnadl

1 Km.

1 ml.

B4413 = B4413 Penygroeslon
Wynnstay

To Sarn

To Bryncroes

42'

42'

'Craig Ewig

Capel Tyddyn

to Botwnnog

Meillionydd

P

radio mast

axe factory

Mynydd Rhiw

To Felin Uchaf

Continued Route 10

To Penccer-au

radar

St Aelrhiw

To Botwnnog

mine (dis.)

Saithbont

To Abersoch

Capel Neigwl

Capel Pisgan

Rhiw

Continued Route 9

To Porth Ysgo

P

Plas yn Rhiw

Porth Neigwl

Mynydd y Craig

Rhiw – Phew

Distance *The run around the hill is nothing, 8km (5mls), with*
a total climb of 205m (680ft).
I am proposing this as a part of a longer run, loops from
Aberdaron, Tudweiliog, Abersoch or further. Taken with a
distance of 20 or 30 kilometres, and depending on which way
round you go, this is probably a grade of 'tough'.

The village of Rhiw straddles the 190m contour (about 600ft), and
at the South end of the village Mynydd y Graig tumbles from its
242m down to the sea. For the cyclist this means two things; the
weather, one moment you're spotting shipping on it's way to
China, the next you're in cloying mist, and secondly hills. Four
roads meet in Rhiw, all of them rise to the village.

Parking
On the flank of the mountain below the axe factory (disused); in
the village near the top chapel; below Plas yn Rhiw; down at
Porthysgo to the south-west, Sarn Mellteyrn to the north and at
the west end of Porth Neigwl (*Hell's Mouth*).

Caravans/Camping
Bryncroes/Llangwnnadl in the north, Botwnnog, Neigwl Ganol
and Treheli in the east, and Aberdaron to the west.

Refreshments
None, the shop closed some years ago, the cafe closed recently.

The Run
Of the four ascents, by far the most difficult is the road from Porth Neigwl, which is steep (20%) for around a kilometre. If you are pushing the bike up here (I have my hand up) why not take the very minor road past Plas yn Rhiw to the old Church of St Aelrhiw (watching out for adders), then it's a simple ride into the village. Less difficult is the minor road on the North end of Mynydd Rhiw, which is as long, but less steep. The two climbs from the Aberdaron side are a breeze in comparison.

The Coast
Dramatic. Two paved roads, both dead ends, wander out onto Mynydd y Graig and Mynydd Penarfynydd, and footpaths run over these hills.

Geology
As far as I can work out, Mynydd y Graig is volcanic, a part of the outpouring of magma from the Earth's interior which also form the high mountains of Snowdonia. Old, but not as old as the rock on the northern coast. Mynydd Rhiw is different, subtly, and contains two rocks which proved useful to two different peoples at two different times; a belt of shale, used in the axe factory, and a huge amount of manganese.

The Axe Factory
On the brow of the hill, mined in shallow pits, the spoil from one being used to fill the last, this factory was Neolithic, C5th to C3rd BC. The axes produced were thin and narrow, finely worked and polished, and used throughout Wales for carving and shaping wood and cutting up animals.

There are lots of other traces of ancient peoples on these hills, hill forts, hut circles, enclosures, burial chambers, and cairns, but, to be honest, you won't see much of them on a bike. Interested? Look up www.rhiw.com.

Plas yn Rhiw

A National Trust house, C17th, splendidly revived and occupied by the three Misses Keating, who helped to resist the tide of C20th development on Llŷn, including the construction of a nuclear power plant at Edern.

MoD Radar Station

Once hush-hush, used to track guided missiles from the now defunct range down the coast at Aberporth.

Plas yn Rhiw

Y 'Rebel' – Barking and chasing is fun

11 Porth Neigwl

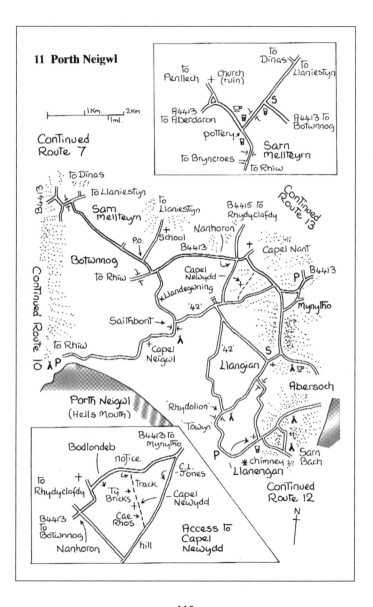

Porth Neigwl (*Hell's Mouth*)

Distance *Family ride 9km (5.5 miles)*

This section is triple purpose. Firstly it's an easy family loop from Porth Neigwl through the villages of Llanengan and Llangian. Secondly, for Popular and Enthusiastic riders, at some time your rides will pass this way. Thirdly, if you have a spare half hour you may wish to take a look at Capel Newydd.

Parking
There is parking at Porth Neigwl. The small car park is almost invariably full, and in the summer there is nearly always an ice cream van here, and sometimes an impromptu mart. selling surfing stuff. Cars park on the verge stretching away on both sides from the car park

There is also a car park at Mynytho.

Caravans/camping
One of the most popular sites is near Porth Neigwl at Rhydolion. There's another at Neigwl Ganol near Saithbont. There's a bunkhouse (Sgubor Unnos) too, at Tanrallt Farm in Llangian (tel 01758 713527).

Refreshments
There's a pub in Llanengan (Sun Inn) and up the hill from Llangian is a caravan site with a tea bar.

The Coast

Porth Neigwl is a four mile long beach of sand and pebbles, popular with surfers (www.westcoastsurf.co.uk/surfreport), there is even a webcam. In the old days it was much feared by seafarers, and there are reports of up to 30 shipwrecks here, including rumours of a French vessel in 1629 lured ashore by wreckers, who then killed and plundered.

The Family Run

Park at Porth Neigwl and wander off left to Tywyn, where it seems there is often a farmer tending to his sheep. Take a left. This is a low lying plateau reclaimed from the marshes in C19th, with fields separated by gorse hedges and countless small bridges over the ditches and streams. Remains can be seen from 1937-1945 when it was used as a grass relief airfield for RAF Penrhos, and a bombing and air to ground gunnery range, with targets floating offshore and moving targets on land, on a looped railway track.

Spin around back through Llangian and Llanengan.

Capel Newydd

The floor is green with undisturbed moss and lichen. On the lectern a bible is slowly turning to earth. It is the earliest surviving Nonconformist chapel in northern Wales, built in 1769.

Llandegwning

The origins of the church are ancient, though the present church was rebuilt in 1840, with an unusual tower. The Church Of Wales was keen to sell off the church for residential use, until it was pointed out that the ancestors of the bones buried beneath the floor may not be too keen. It is now in community use.

Botwnnog

Henry Rowlands, Bishop of Bangor, was born in Mellteyrn, and his will made provision, on his death in 1616 for a school at Botwnnog, built two years later. By 1830 there was still not much to the village, a Calvinistic chapel (Capel Rhyd-Bach) at one end; the smithy, near the present Pont y Gof at the other; and a small complex around the church. At the end of the Century, a new school had been built, and the shop/ post office and two other houses at the crossroads. Efail Pont y Gof remains a traditional single-storey crogloft cottage.

Sarn Mellteyrn

At some time on your travels, you'll end up in Sarn, and you'll wonder how best to leave. My partner, Annie, asks me every time, what is the best way out of Sarn? and I do that French thing where you blow through your lips and they vibrate, flubberflubberflubber, as if I can pluck an easy route out of thin air.

The main road, the B4413 to Aberdaron, is steepest at the bottom, the worst bit is at the bend and then it continues to rise for another mile or so. The minor road to Penllech is definitely easier, if you're going that way, towards the underpass for cows, and the cromlech.

The road to Dinas is really steep at the bottom, then eases off into a steady climb up to the Capel Brynmawr.

Going southwards, there is a choice between the straightforward climb up towards Rhiw, steep, then a steady climb of 135m (450ft), or you can turn left immediately after the bridge and take the (secret) back road to Bryncroes. The first bit is tough and often greasy (i.e. wheel spin), but after that it never seems so bad to me (although it is still an ascent of 128m (420ft).

Of course the B4413 to Botwnnog is a piece of cake, but I'm assuming you've come that way.

Sarn is a funny little place. There used to be an auction mart here, and before that two annual hiring fairs. It still has three pubs, though it is unusual for them all to be open at the same time due to domestic dramas. There's a garage and two shops and a cafe and a pottery run by Oldrich Asenbyl who throws pots with one arm, all packed into a slim valley.

The climb to Rhiw from Aberdaron

A rest by the chapel at Rhiw

After a hard day in the saddle

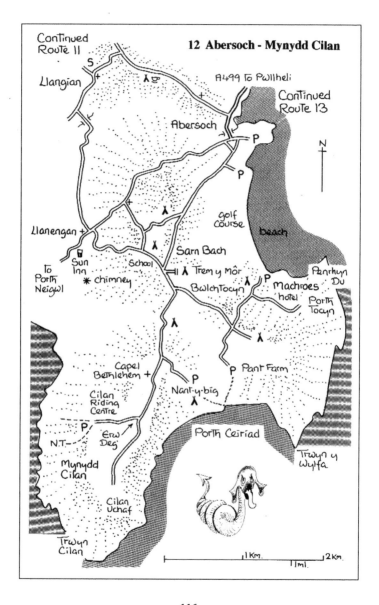

12 Abersoch - Mynydd Cilan

Continued Route 11

Llangian

A499 To Pwllheli

Continued Route 13

Abersoch

P

P

N

golf course

beach

Llanengan

Sun Inn

School

Sarn Bach

Trem y Môr

chimney

Bwlch Tocyn

P

Machroes hotel

Penrhyn Du

To Porth Neigwl

Porth Tocyn

Capel Bethlehem

P

Pant Farm

Cilan Riding Centre

Nant-y-big

P

N.T.

Erw Deg

Porth Ceiriad

Mynydd Cilan

Cilan Uchaf

Trwyn y Wylfa

Trwyn Cilan

1 Km.

2 Km.

1 ml.

116

Route 12

Abersoch, Mynydd Cilan

Distance *Abersoch to Mynydd Cilan is 5Km (3mls), but this is more an exploratory thing.*

Grade *Neither one thing nor the other.*

Links *I would make this my destination from somewhere else on Llŷn.*

Geographers describe Porth Neigwl (*Hells Mouth*) as a high-energy environment, wave action both eroding the beach and feeding it by eroding the cliffs at the Western end, cliffs made from material dropped by retreating ice. All this activity is overseen by the solid bulk of Mynydd Cilan.

This is also true of today's frenetic human activity. The headland looks down upon the surfers and wake boarders, the caravanners and bucket and spaders.

Cilan head is not natural cycling country. For a start it's all hills, and every which way you go, you end up at the sea. On the other hand, it's not natural car-driving country either. The lanes are narrow more often than not, and you can find yourself spending half a day cooped up in a hot car reversing for caravans or tractors or the vans of professional grass-cutters. So use the bike to climb the hill, lock it to a fence and explore the last half mile or so on foot, and the high headland of Mynydd Cilan, and the beach at Porth Ceiriad are both well worth it.

Parking
Abersoch
Machroes, Bwlchtocyn, and Pant Farm (for Porth Ceiriad)
Nant-y-big (for Porth Ceiriad)
Mynydd Cilan (near the riding stables)
Porth Neigwl

Caravans/Camping This is caravan/camping heaven, choice without number.

Refreshments
Cafe's and pubs in Abersoch.
The Sun Inn at Llanengan.
Porth Tocyn Country House Hotel has an award-winning restaurant.

The Coast
Cilan Head is a headland of contrast. The beaches of Abersoch are a popular holiday destination, and the bay is a boating and water sport centre. Porth Ceiriad is a beautiful sandy beach, backed by fascinating rock formations. Buried in the sand is the wreck of the 'Franchise', which ran aground in 1855 in thick fog with a cargo of cotton. The headland of Trwyn Cilan and Mynydd Cilan has various SSSI's, noted for the colourful flora, chamomile, pale dog-violet, pill wort, ivy broomrape etc, and the seabirds, including chough and an auk colony of razorbill and guillemot. There used to be a population of red kite here, are they here still?

Abersoch
Abersoch is a busy holiday village, a centre for sailing, surfing and other water sports. When I say 'busy', in summer I mean really busy. In June it hosts the Abersoch Jazz Festival, in July the

Wakeboard Festival, and in August the Regatta.

In recent years there was a sense of shock when, in 2003 a 2mx3m beach hut with a corrugated iron roof sold for £39,500; in 2005 a plot of sand big enough for a beach hut sold for £63,000; and in 2008 a beach hut measuring 3mx4m sold for £85,000. It came with a freehold parcel of sand.

Llangian

A stone can be seen near the church, split in half by an earthquake in 1858.

The Church of St Cian is partly C13th, and the roof is C15th. In the churchyard is a rough stone pillar, it's head cut away to make a sundial, the Latin inscription reads, *Meli Medici Fili Martini Iacit*. (The stone) of Melus, the Doctor, son of Martinus. He lies (here). This is C5th or early C6th, and is the only record in Britain of a doctor on early Christian inscriptions. Such details were normal on pagan Roman epitaphs, but the early Christians thought themselves above such earthly matters.

Llanengan

The Church, late C15th and early C16th had connections with St Mary's Abbey on Ynys Enlli, and was a popular place of pilgrimage.

Llanengan church

The Metal Mines

Beneath these headlands lead, copper and the ores of iron and manganese have been mined intermittently for Centuries. The mines were probably opened initially in the 1630's when Thomas Bushell, lessor of the Mines Royal in North Wales, was scouring the Principality for silver for the coins of the Royal Mint in Aberystwyth.

Restored mine chimney at Llanengan

Penrhyn Du was first, worked for silver-lead and lead ore for the next 250 years. Most of the buildings and the massive waste tips have disappeared, and the workings were blocked up and flooded before 1900. At the South end of St Tudwal's Roads (Bay) are the beds of tramways, portals of levels, sites of engine-houses and mine offices, shafts, the reservoir and rows of cottages. Most of the land here is private property and there's not much to see without trespassing. The ore was exported from a purpose-built quay.

The mine at Tan yr Allt and Port Nigel across the peninsula, was more recent. The shafts go down 80/90 fathoms, and in 1878 a 40 inch cylinder Cornish pumping engine was installed to keep the water out, but the water won and the mine shut in 1893. At it's peak the Pantgwny mine employed 301 men (boys under 12 were banned from working underground in 1878. There were the usual accidents, rock falls and misfired explosives, but, on 17 Feb 1885, when 3 men were drowned working at 60 fathoms, it took two months to get the bodies out, and an accident site inspection was not possible until September (and we think we have it tough with the rain today).

The tall chimney at Porth Nigel, standing over the remnants of the mine buildings, was restored in the late 1990's.

St Tudwals's Islands

Saint Tudwal, AD 528 to 564, was one of the sons of King Howell Mawr, King of Brittany, who fought alongside King Arthur, and may have been one of the Knights of the Round Table. He founded a sanctuary on the eastern island, before moving to Brittany to become Bishop of Treguier. In C13th the sanctuary was enlarged to a Priory, but this was wrecked in a storm in1887. Now the islands are breeding grounds to razorbill, guillemot, kittiwake and cormorant. A plan to turn an island into a nudist colony failed.

Climbing to Rhiw

13 At Play with the Igneous Intrusions

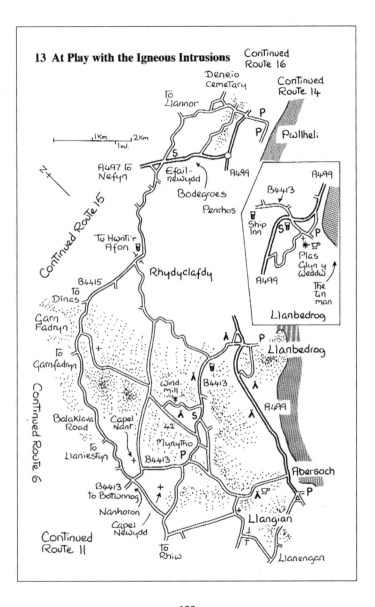

Continued Route 16

Continued Route 14

Deneio Cemetary

To Llannor

Pwllheli

P

P

1Km. 2Km
1ml.

A497 To Nefyn

S

Efail-newydd

A499

Continued Route 15

Bodegroes

Penrhos

B4413

A499

Ship Inn

S

P

Plas Glyn y Weddw

The Tin man

A499

Llanbedrog

To Hwnt i'r Afon

Rhydyclafdy

B4415
To Dinas

Garn Fadryn

To Garnfadryn

Llanbedrog

P

A499

B4413

Wind-mill

Balaklava Road

Capel Nant

42

S

Mynytho

P

B4413

To Llaniestyn

Abersoch

P

B4413 to Botwnnog

Nanhoron

Capel Newydd

Llangian

Llanengan

Continued Route 11

To Rhiw

Continued Route 6

At play with the Igneous Intrusions: Pwllheli to Mynytho

Distance *Pwllheli to Llanengan and back – 32km (20mls).*

Grade *Popular (Medium)*

Other runs are possible here, there is plenty of choice, for longer or shorter runs. Routes 6, 11 or 15 could also be incorporated for more variation.

A line of igneous intrusions have survived as a series of four or five hills, from the unmistakable Garn Fadryn, to Garn Bach, Garn Saethon, Carneddol, Foel Faen (with it's disused windmill, known locally as the 'Pot Jam') to Mynydd Tirycwmwd above Llanbedrog. This route begins and ends in Pwllheli, and plays around with these hills. There are ups and downs, and I'll point out the steepest ones.

Firstly a word about the A499, Abersoch – Llanbedrog coastal road. It can be a busy road, and no fun to cycle on. The stretch to Llanbedrog is OK, but after that, over the marshes to Pwllheli, it becomes narrow and bolshie. If you do ride any of this road, you'll notice, when you leave, how everything slows down, the traffic, your pulse, the world, and you notice once more, the hovering kestrel.

Otherwise, the chunkiest stretches of hill are the B4413 out of

Llanbedrog to Mynytho, and the narrow lane out of Llanbedrog over Mynydd Tirycwmwd. It's a climb also onto the ridge from Abersoch, and from Llangian, and up the minor road from Llandegwning to Mynytho.

Enjoy playing around up here, the views are stunning.

Parking
Pwllheli, Llanbedrog and Abersoch, it goes without saying, although in summer Abersoch can jam up with cars. There's a car park at Mynytho, and you can park down at Porth Neigwl.

Caravans/camping
Lots of places along the coast.

Refreshments
Again, you're looking at Pwllheli, Llanbedrog (the Gallery at Plas Glyn y Weddw has a tea room) and Abersoch. A campsite up the hill from Abersoch has a small cafe. In addition, there's The Sun Inn at Llanengan, and Tu Hwnt i'r Afon at Rhydyclafdy. (Tu hwnt i'r Afon – *the other side of the river*).

Efailnewydd
Positioned at the convergence of two drovers roads, this was an ideal place for a smithy (*efail:* smithy). The huge house on the corner used to be the Farmers Arms.

Llanbedrog
Pedrog, a Cornish missionary, arrived in AD C5th/C6th and established a Llan. The present church dates from C16th, and doubled up as a stables for Cromwell in the Civil War.

Up on the hill the famous tin man (iron man) was originally a ship's figurehead placed here by Soloman Andrews. When it was

Plas Glyn y Weddw – Art Gallery and Cafe

vandalised by fire, Mr Simon van de Put, a local artist, constructed a replacement from recycled steel, and manhandled it up here in 1980. When that decayed, a replacement, made by Berwyn Jones, David and Hugh Jones, was helicoptered up here in 2002. Being hollow, it sings in the wind.

Plas Glyn y Weddw was built in 1856 by the family from Madryn, but the whole estate was sold in 1896, and with it 90% of Llanbedrog. The area was, at that time, known as the Cambrian Riviera. Soloman Andrews, a Cardiff businessman, turned the Hall into an art gallery, and built a horse-drawn tram service from Pwllheli.

Pwllheli Market, held on the Maes every Wednesday

Hafan Pwllheli – the sailing marina in the old harbour

Nanhoron

The estate has been in the possession of the Edwards family for 700 years. Centred on the Regency mansion at the crossroads, pride is taken in the quality of the estate management. The family were Nonconformists, and built two chapels; Capel Nant, established in 1782 (the present building dates from 1877), and Capel Newydd, built in 1769, the oldest surviving Nonconformist chapel in northern Wales.

Penrhos

In 1936 it was decided to site an RAF bombing school at Penyberth (Penrhos). In protest at the London Government's military takeover of land of heritage importance, the Welsh Nationalists burned down a hangar. Nonetheless, the base began operating in 1937, and in 1940 suffered six Luftwaffe raids. No 312 (Czech) Squadron was moved in to protect the base, and RAF Hells Mouth upgraded too. After the War, part of the site was sold to the Polish Housing Society to house Eastern European service personnel.

14 Pwllheli

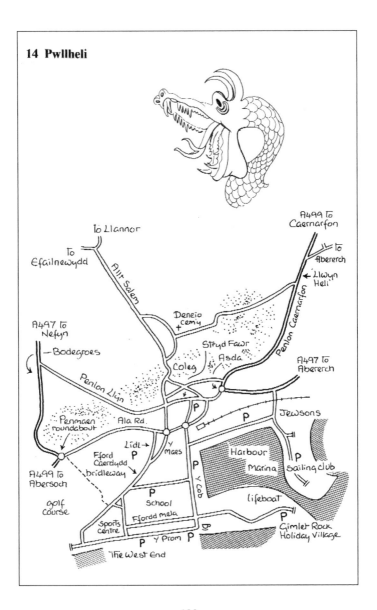

Pwllheli

This is not really a route, but a guide to cycling in and out of Pwllheli. It's quite exciting really, for the town, a page to itself. For most of Llŷn, Pwllheli is the town, with a cinema, theatre, most of the shops, the market, the college. Most buses come here, and it's where the youth of Llŷn hang out. There is no bypass for Pwllheli, and as a consequence, especially in summer, and especially on market day (Wednesday) or when Wakestock is on, traffic backs up to get through, and the main shopping streets, Stryd Fawr, Gaol Street and around Y Maes (market place) become jammed up. In summer also the Marina and the Sailing Club become packed with boaters.

Though you may not be aware of it at first, Pwllheli is very Welsh, and fights hard to preserve it's Welsh-ness. One or two shopkeepers will address you in Welsh, even though you are obviously a visitor. The use of a couple of words in reply goes a long way.

It is also not immediately apparent, but Pwllheli is backed by a small ridge which runs from Penlon Llŷn to Penlon Caernarfon. So, if you are using the back roads (through Deneio) into the town, be aware that it's a bit up and down. The A497 to Abererch and Cricieth can be busy, but is wide. You can avoid much of the traffic in town by using the harbour road from Jewsons to the railway station. The bridleway from the Penmaen roundabout towards the school and promenade is cycleable.

Pwllheli

As a market town, it is old. The Charter was granted back in 1355 by the Black Prince (Edward III of England). The town also has a long maritime tradition. Hundreds of sailing vessels have been built here, the last one around 1880. The harbour has silting problems, and has been thoroughly dredged over the years. It is officially recognised as a European Centre for Sailing, though plans for further expansion of the marina have met resistance from those who fear the inevitable influx of English would water down the Welsh-ness of Pwllheli. They have a point, after all, Plaid Cymru (the Party of Wales) was formed here in 1925.

Tourism came with the railway. The station was built in 1869, and extended to its present site to give better access to the West End. In 1890 Soloman Andrews began to develop the shoreline here, with an hotel, apartments and promenade. He built a horse-drawn tramway from the West End to his new arts complex at Plas Glyn y Weddw in Llanbedrog. This operated until 1927.

Pwllheli, where the youth of Llŷn hang out

Summer's day above Porth Neigwl

Llandegwning church

15 Gors Geirch

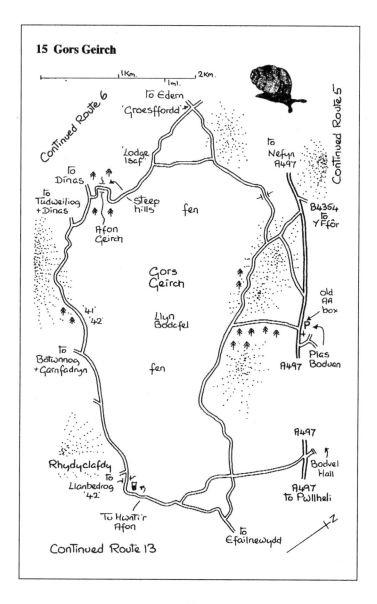

1Km. 2Km.
1ml.

To Edern
'Groesffordd'

Continued Route 6

'Lodge Isaf'

To Dinas

To Tudweiliog + Dinas

Afon Geirch

Steep hills

fen

Gors Geirch

Llyn Bodfel

'41' '42'

To Botwnnog + Garnfadryn

fen

Rhydyclafdy
To Llanbedrog
'42'

Tu Hwnt'r Afon

To Nefyn
A497

Continued Route 5

B4354
To Y Ffôr

old AA box

P

Plas Boduan

A497

A497

Bodvel Hall

A497
To Pwllheli

To Efailnewydd

Continued Route 13

132

Gors Geirch Circular
Corsydd Llŷn (Llŷn Fenland)

Distance *13km (8mls)*

Grade *On its own this is really a long family run, it is all on quiet roads. As a popular run it's easy, but it's one of those, like Garn Fadryn, which you'll use as a loop on a longer run.*

I'm describing here the loop around Gors Geirch. There are limited opportunities to park on the loop itself, and in all probability you'll use it as part of a longer ride. The route meanders and undulates, under the watchful eye of the hill forts on Garn Fadryn and Garn Boduan. It is subtle, peek-a-boo country, and every now and then you come up for air. The steepest climbs are out of the river valley over the Afon Geirch, a climb of 50m (165ft) both sides.

Hardly any of the road junctions are signposted, but you'll notice that if you keep taking lefts (or rights, obviously) you'll keep going round and round in circles.

Parking
The best place is by the old AA box on the A497. You can also squeeze your car in at the bottom of the track up Garn Boduan, and there's a wide roadside verge below Rhydyclafdy.

Refreshments
Pubs at Rhydyclafdy, Morfa Nefyn, Edern and Nefyn.

Gors Geirch is the largest of a chain of four rich fen sites, described as a sinuous valley mire system. Gors Geirch formed as peat slowly filled a lake left over after the Ice Age, when ice sheets from Ireland, from the north and from Snowdonia moved south over Llŷn, dropping stuff on the way. Llyn Bodafen is all that remains of the lake. The fen is fed by calcium rich springs. It is a mosaic of sphagnum moss and rare sedges, with many special plants including orchids, and insects including the Marsh Fritillary butterfly, dragonflies, damselflies, and, notably, the very rare Desmoulin's Whorl snail, and Geyer's Whorl snail. It covers the valley bottom from the base of Garn Boduan to Rhydyclafdy.

Of course access is limited, and, being on a bike, you'll find it hard to admire the water snails or even see them, but at least you'll know they are there, and it shows that Llŷn is not just a stretch of golden beaches and towering cliffs.

It is also a 'rejuvenated' landscape. You'll notice the extraction from sand pits. These were beaches before the land rose, or the sea fell, or both, forcing the Afon Geirch, to recut it's passage to the sea, hence the steep hills on either side of the new valley.

Milestone *Ash tree at Plas Talhenbont*

Farm at Tai'n Lôn

16 Pennarth Fawr

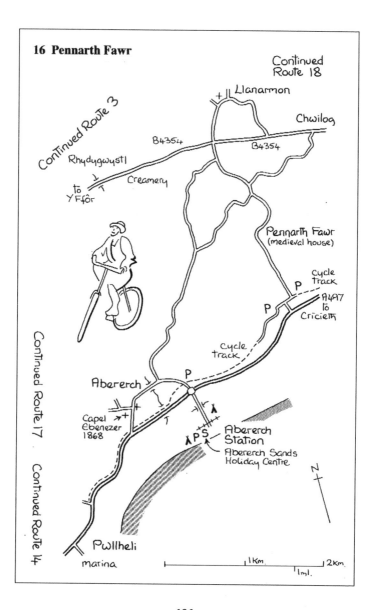

Continued Route 18

Llanarmon

Chwilog

Continued Route 3

B4354

B4354

Rhydygwystl

to Y Ffôr

Creamery

Pennarth Fawr
(medieval house)

Cycle Track

P

P
P

A497 to Criciceth

Cycle Track

Abererch

P

Capel Ebenezer 1868

P S

Abererch Station

Abererch Sands Holiday Centre

N

Continued Route 17

Continued Route 14

Pwllheli marina

1 Km.   2 Km.

1 ml.

136

Pennarth Fawr
Abererch – Pennarth Fawr – Abererch

Distance *7km (4mls)*

This is an easy family run. It can also be used as a destination, for these are quiet roads which can be factored into longer runs. It is included in Route 17, it could be part of Routes 3 and 18 too.

This is undramatic country, flattish, oak-lined lanes winding through cattle country. These are the cows which give you milk and cheese, via the nearby creamery. Alongside the improved A497 cyclists have been given the old, traffic-free road to play with. Abererch is sleepy too, the shop closed 10 years ago. To get to Abererch Station you'll need to negotiate the roundabout on the A497, but beyond Abererch Station is access to the beach, and the Holiday Centre (ice cream in the shop).

To get to this run from Pwllheli, you can use the main road to Abererch, which is wide, but fast. The pavement is being widened to include a cycle path. There is also a back roads way, past the Deneio cemetery, with a small section of the A499 before you branch off right, emerging at the Capel Ebenezer in Abererch. There are a few ups and downs on this route.

Parking
At Abererch Station, and also at a couple of places on the old main road.

Camping/Caravans
Abererch Station.

The Coast
Wide, sandy beach.

Pennarth Fawr (Tŷ Canoloesol/ Medieval House)
This house is a rare survivor of a medieval home, built by Hywel ap Madog about 1460. It is open all year, with free entry, but no cafe.

Abererch
An ancient township/village grouped around the Church of St Cawrdaf, on a bend in the river. It remained little changed until the end of the C18th. With both a Calvinistic Methodist chapel, and then the Congregational Ebenezer chapel built in 1868, the village more than doubled in size in C19th. The church was first recorded in the C13th, and was extended and improved over the next few centuries.

Pennarth Fawr – a medieval hall

The Rivers of the Eastern peninsula

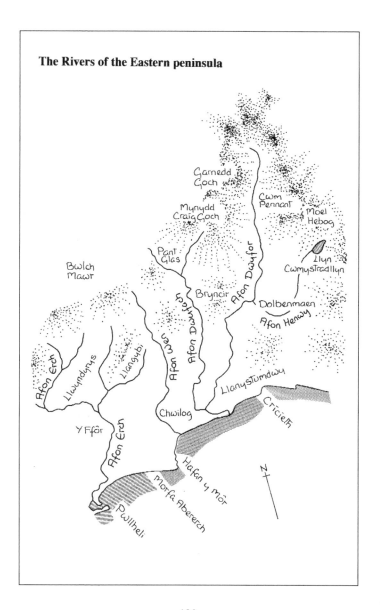

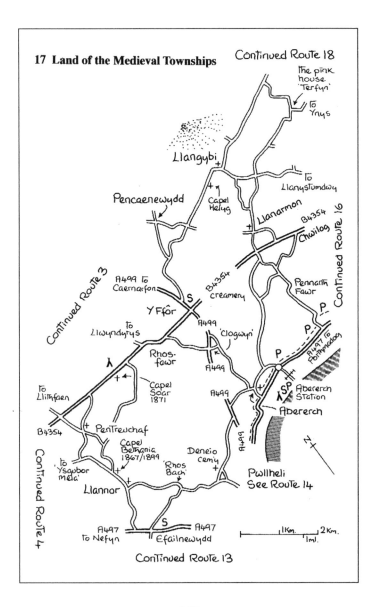

17 Land of the Medieval Townships

Continued Route 18

The pink house 'Terfyn'

To Ynys

Llangybi

To Llanystumdwy

Pencaenewydd

Capel Helyg

Llanarmon

B4354

Chwilog

Continued Route 16

A499 To Caernarfon

Continued Route 3

B4354 creamery

Pennarth Fawr

P

Y Ffôr

S

A499

'Clogwyn'

P

To Llwyndyrys

P

A497 To Porthmadog

Rhos-fawr

A499

P

SP

Abererch Station

To Llithfaen

Capel Soar 1871

A499

Abererch

B4354

PenTrewchaf

Deneio cemy

A499

Pwllheli
See Route 14

Capel Bethania 1867/1899

Rhos Bach

To 'Ysgubor Mela'

Llannor

N

Continued Route 4

A497 To Nefyn

S

A497

Efailnewydd

1Km. 2Km.
1ml.

Continued Route 13

140

The Land of the Medieval Townships
Pwllheli – Llangybi – Llannor – Pwllheli

Distance *30km (19mls)*

Grade *Popular (Easy, in comparison)*

All adjoining Routes can be used to extend the ride.

This is dreamy pastureland, a land of don't-let-Stanley-get-too-far-ahead-we'll-never-see-him-again. "Where are we?" Annie and her sisters would cry from the back seat of the ancient fish-smelling Studebaker sedan, as they drove from the coast into America. Annie's father would put on his most lugubrious face and say, "We're hopelessly lost." On the other hand, it's flat(ish), it's lush, it's good country for cycling, sooner or later you'll discover where you are, and by the by, you'll find a cure for the blind and the lame.

Parking
Pwllheli and Abererch. There is some parking too on the B4354, at Chwilog , near the Creamery and on the roadside in the woodland West of Rhosfawr.

Caravans/Camping
Abererch Station, and to the west of Y Ffôr.

Refreshments

There's the Madryn Arms in Chwilog, otherwise there's nothing until you reach Pwllheli.

The Run

Leave town on the A497 Porthmadog road, picking up the cycle path at Abererch. Turn left to Pennarth Fawr, and on to Llanarmon. Do the loop around via the 'pink house' and back to Llangybi. Then it's back to Y Ffôr, right on the B4354 for a couple of miles, through Rhosfawr, and left to Llannor. Work the side roads to slip into Pwllheli through the back door. Lovely.

The Landscape

The first thing to say is that what you see is not a medieval landscape. Two hundred years ago this land was 'enclosed' and transformed

Abererch church

Llannor church

into the fields and hedgerows you see today. It is also wet, there are numerous ditches and streams draining mostly into Afon Erch, hence it's suitability for pasture. Imagine the landscape pre-drainage, and you'll have the medieval landscape, plus, of course, lots more woodland and scrub, and without the roads. The settlement pattern was the same though (without the large farms dating also from the Enclosures), and these villages were quasi-monastic medieval townships. The names are a giveaway too. So who were these Saints?

St Cawrdaf (of Abererch) was born in AD 495 and became King of Fferreg (a bit of Gwent). He was, apparently, a wise monarch, a counsellor to King Arthur and the father of 'several saintly children', and his feast day is 5th December. What more do you need to know?

St Cybi Felyn (Llangybi) AD 483-555 was a different kettle of fish. He was trouble. A Cornishman who rejected politics for the calling, he began his travels around the Celtic world founding

Ffynnon Gybi, near Llangybi

churches in southern Wales and Ireland, without being welcomed in either. He then crossed back to Llŷn where he angered the local King Maelgwn Gwynedd when the latter found St Cybi establishing an unauthorised Christian community here. They must have reached an accommodation, for all turned out well in the end and he was buried on Ynys Enlli (sounds like a Panto doesn't it?). The man was especially known for having his face to the sun, and so cultivating an enviable tan.

St Garmon (Llanarmon) is a mystery man. Was he St Germanus of Auxerre who visited Britain in AD 429; or was he St Gorman of the Isle of Man over here on a package tour; or was he St Gorman, the Benedictine Bishop of Schleswig in Denmark, who first brought over a black an white cow? Perhaps we'll never know.

The medieval church of Llannor is dedicated to the Holy Cross. They played it safe in Llannor.

Llangybi

There are several medieval healing wells in this area, and perhaps Ffynnon Gybi (*ffynnon*: well) is the most evocative. Through the churchyard, over the stile in the far corner, down the field and over the footbridge. It's a tranquil, curious place. The use of wells for curing ailments is medieval. At the end of C18th the fashionable success of the waters at Bath led to the commissioning of a report on the curative properties of the waters here, which so impressed the Vicar of Llanystumdwy that he persuaded the landowners to provide conveniences and amenities. The main well-chamber could be older, but the buildings are probably mid C18th. The cottage was used by those taking the cure, which involved drinking and bathing, and could last a week, but the waters were said to be able to cure blindness, fevers and lameness. Who needs the NHS?

Nearby, along the road to Pencaenewydd is Capel Helyg, one of the oldest independent chapels in northern Wales, originally built in 1652, and rebuilt in 1877, it served the Congregationalists.

Near Llanystumdwy

Lloyd George Museum

A Tale of Two Afonydd
Afon Wen and Afon Dwyfach, from
Llanystumdwy and Chwilog

Distance *23km (15mls)*

Grade *Popular (Easy, in comparison)*

This run could link in nicely with any of the surrounding Routes.

This is one of those runs. When the Belgians in the next caravan ask "Where have you been today?", you think, where have I been? And did it begin with an L or a Y?

The Afon Wen begins life on the slopes of Bwlch Mawr, above Clynnog Fawr. The Afon Dwyfach drains the slopes of Mynydd Craig Goch on the other side of Clynnog. They run Southwards parallel to each other, and both empty into the sea on the long pebbly/sandy beach between Cricieth and The Haven. This patch of country also contains the disused railway line between Afonwen and Bryncir, and Lôn Goed, both of which should, in an ideal world, be of use to a cyclist, but neither is. What you get instead is beautifully gentle cycling through mixed woodland/farmland with the smell of hay and bog myrtle. Llanystumdwy is a fine place to start and finish.

18 A Tale of Two Afonydd

To Llanarmon

Glan y Wern

B4354

Capel Uchaf

Madryn Arms

Madryn Villa

S

P

To Porthmadog

To Afonwen

Chwilog

Continued Route 2

To Clynnog

To Pencaenewydd

31

To Bryncir

Bryn Engan

Tiny road easy to miss

Continued Route 17

The pink house 'Terfyn'

to Ynys

Ffynnon Gybi

Llangybi

'Penbryn'

Capel Helyg

'Felin Pencoed'

To Pencaenewydd

'31a'

'31a'

Llanarmon

B4354 To Y Ffôr

Glan y Wern

To Pennarth Fawr

Capel Uchaf

S

Chwilog

A497

Afonwen

N

Continued Route 17

Hafan y Môr

A497 To Pwllheli

1 Km. 2 Km.

1 ml.

148

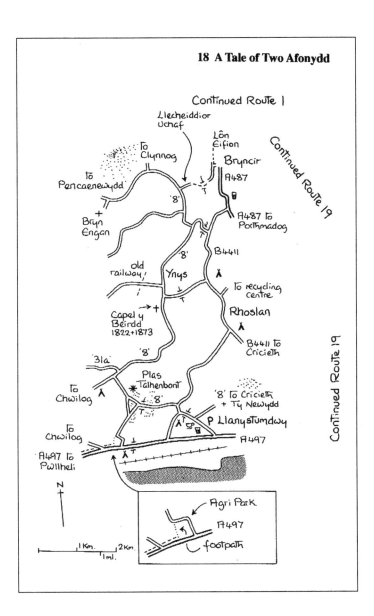

18 A Tale of Two Afonydd

Continued Route 1

Llecheiddior Uchaf

Lôn Eifion

Bryncir
A487

To Clynnog

To Pencaenewydd

Bryn Engan

Continued Route 19

A487 To Porthmadog

'8'

'8' B4411

old railway

Ynys

To recycling centre

Rhoslan

Capel y Beirdd 1822+1873

B4411 To Cricieth

'31a'

'8'

Plas Talhenbont

'8'

'8' To Cricieth + Tŷ Newydd

To Chwilog

Continued Route 19

P Llanystumdwy

To Chwilog

A497

A497 To Pwllheli

N

Agri Park

A497

footpath

1 Km.   2 Km.
1 ml.

149

Parking
Llanystumdwy has a large car park. There's one in Chwilog too, opposite the Madryn Arms.

Caravans/Camping
Again, Tyddyn Sadler Llanystumdwy is your spot, and also at Bont Fechan, a little ways to the west along the A497, plus a fairly obscure one at Tyddyn Heilyn/Tyddyn Cwcwallt.

Refreshments
Llanystumdwy –Tafarn y Plu
Chwilog – Madryn Arms
The clincher for me is the Caffi Dwyfor, a lovely cafe on the riverbank in Llanystumdwy.

The Run
From Llanystumdwy follow Sustrans' Route 8 over the Afon Dwyfach, up the steep bank on the other side, with Plas Talhenbont on your left, then north past Capel y Beirdd, and past Llecheiddior Uchaf farm (where Route 8 turns off to seek Lôn Eifion, the railway path). Take the next left. This next bit of road is worth the whole trip, with a tasty spread before your eyes, down over the valleys of the 'Afonydd' to the sea. Turn left onto the Pencaenewydd road and then almost immediately left again onto the tiniest of roads with grass growing in the centre (it's easy to miss). This takes you gently down in and out of forestry and you can then either return through Llangybi and Chwilog, or entirely on minor roads back to Plas Talhenbont and Llanystumdwy.

Llanystumdwy
"Lloyd George knew my father; my father knew Lloyd George", sung endlessly to the tune of 'Onward Christian Soldiers' around camp fires. Ah, happy days(!). Some say it referred to his

womanising. No, I can't figure that one out either. The great man moved here as a baby, with his mother, to stay with his uncle Richard Lloyd, shoemaker and Baptist minister, and under his influence developed as a radical, nationalist and Nonconformist. He was Prime Minister from 1916 to 1922 and held the Caernarfonshire seat in Westminster for 55 years. We have L-G to thank for the state pension. The museum will tell you more.

His grave (on the side road to Cricieth) was designed by Sir Clough Williams-Ellis, as was Capel Moriah, the museum gates and the library window at Tŷ Newydd, now the National Writers Centre in Wales.

Afonwen

There's not much here, but there is access to the coast, and you can make out the remnants of the railway station. This was where the Caernarfon line joined the existing railway. There were three platforms, a licensed refreshment room and 17 passenger trains each way per day. Workers from the factories of Lancashire and the Midlands mingled here for the first time before spending a week together under the watchful eye of the redcoats in Butlins. It was closed in 1964 by Dr Beeching.

Afonwen is also the start of Y Lôn Goed (the tree-lined lane) which stretches 8 km inland from the coast. It was built in the early C19th to link the farms of the Talhenbont estate and enable the transport of sand and lime to the farms from Afonwen beach. It's a walking route nowadays.

Plas Talhenbont

Built in 1607 by William Vaughan, the estate used to be the largest single owned piece of land in Eifionydd, though it has changed hands and configurations many times over the years. At the time of writing, it could be yours for £2m.

Plas Talhenbont

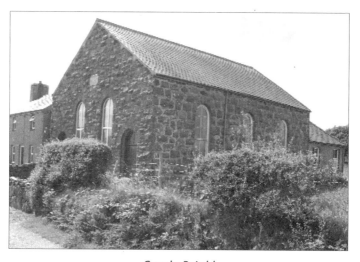

Capel y Beirdd

The Haven (Hafan y Mor)

Further down the coast is the Haven. The camp used to be *H M S Glendower*, a gunnery training 'ship', of which many ex-sailors, including the Duke of Edinburgh, have 'fond' memories. (www.butlinsmemories.com/pwllheli). Before that Billy Butlin built a recruitment assessment camp for the Royal Navy, and afterwards he added the site to his growing holiday camp empire. It was later renamed Wonderworld West, and had a horribly intense loop-the-loop roller coaster (my stomach churns with the memory).

Capel y Beirdd (Chapel of the Bards)

Memorials to the C18th poet Robert ap Gwilym Ddu, and Dewi Wyn o Eifion.

Tŵr Bryncir

Two Royal Seats
Cricieth – Dolbenmaen – Llanllyfni – Cricieth

Distance 40km (25mls)

There are other runs to be enjoyed, both long and short, using Lôn Eifion. I've discussed these in Routes 1 and 24.

Grade Popular (At least a medium), verging on the Enthusiast.

It was August bank holiday Monday, the sun was shining, Cricieth was throbbing with pastels, pitching and putting and cornets, and the A487 was busy with traffic going somewhere else. Apart from Cricieth and the half a dozen cars on the B4411, I didn't meet a single car on this run. Tell a lie, I did meet one, an old chap in a mucky white van, parked up and snoozing, waiting for an acquaintance to come by for a natter (as is common in Llŷn). There have been glory days here, but it's been a while, and now it makes a varied, intriguing cycle run, not one to be rushed. As always there are hills, quite a few ups and downs as a matter of fact, and the high point is 220m (700ft), but this is all in the first half. It would be wrong to say it's all downhill after the interval, but it's not far off. Unless, of course, you go around backwards.

Parking

Cricieth, Llanystumdwy. Also, there's a car park at the end of the cycle path at Bryncir, and parking too in Dolbenmaen, Garndolbenmaen and Llanllyfni.

Caravans/Camping

There's a site in Llanystumdwy and a half a dozen sites around Rhoslan. Plus a sleeping barn at Tyddyn Morthwyl, Cricieth (tel 01766 522115).

Refreshments

Pubs and cafe's in Cricieth and Llanystumdwy. There's a pub in Garndolbenmaen (the Crossfoxes), and the Goat Inn, south of Bryncir, and possibly a cafe at Pant Glas.

The Coast

I can see why Cricieth is popular for holidays. It's an old-fashioned sort of place, but all the ingredients are there.

The Run

How to leave Cricieth. Few cyclists use the A497. I've seen cyclists on the footpaths (both ways), and these are being widened for the use of cyclists. Pedestrians should be given the right of way. The alternative is to climb the hill. It's a climb of 70m (240ft) in just over a kilometre, i.e. it's a bog standard hill. The B4411 has a little traffic, the narrow Lôn Fel doesn't.

For this route, we begin by climbing the hill, and then follow the B4411 for a couple of kilometres. When you reach the Cricieth Caravan Park, turn right. The 'Artists Studio, Clay Sculpture' is at Plas Ymwlch, a Georgian

Y Maes, Cricieth

19 Two Royal Seats

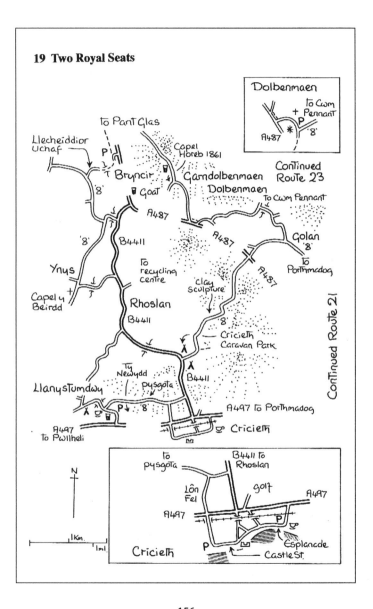

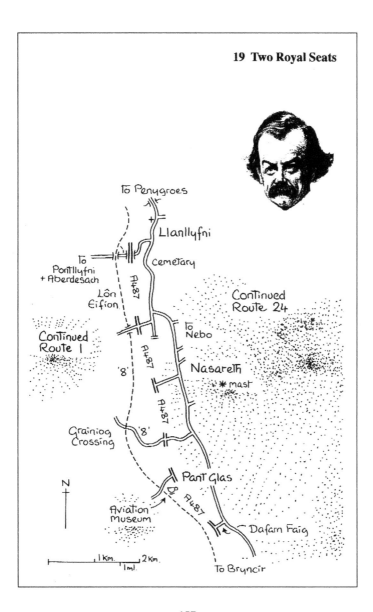

To Penygroes

Llanllyfni

To
Pontllyfni
+ Aberdesach

Cemetary

A487

Lôn
Eifion

Continued
Route 24

Continued
Route 1

To
Nebo

'8'

A487

Nasareth

* mast

A487

Grainiog
Crossing

'8'

N

Pant Glas

A487

Aviation
Museum

A487

Dafarn Faig

1 Km.   2 Km.
1 ml.

To Bryncir

manor house. This is a lovely, single-track road through a wooded landscape. Turn left at Golan, another pleasant run through to Dolbenmaen. You're following Sustrans Route 8, otherwise known as Lôn Las Cymru, Holyhead to Cardiff. In Dolbenmaen the church looks rather sorry for itself, and is a relatively recent building, and the Manor House hides itself away. The real star is that motley looking mound covered with trees behind the disused farm buildings. By C12th, this mound held a castle which was the administrative centre of Eifionydd, and one of the royal courts of the Princes of Gwynedd. From time to time the Prince and his entourage would tour his kingdom on a circuit, both to show his authority and to make any decisions necessary. Llywelyn ap Iorwerth (*Llywelyn the Great*), in about 1230 moved his Eifionydd HQ from this tump to the newly built Cricieth Castle, for a sea view, and to be closer to Cadwalder's ice cream.

There are plenty of short cuts available on this run. The first is the minor road past the recycling centre. It involves a tiny bit of A487, with fast, sometimes heavy traffic, for whom you hardly exist. It also passes Ystumcegid, a small mansion known in the Middle Ages for the generosity of it's hospitality for poets. Regular visitors included Llywelyn ap y Moel who wrote about exciting times when he was embedded with Owain Glyndŵr's' rebel fighters.

Route 8 takes the old post road through Garndolbenmaen, sleepy home to the pub the Cross Foxes and the recording studio in which Pep Le Pew and Gwyneth Glyn laid down their grooves. The road climbs and falls and climbs again, past Dafarn Faig and a roadside cemetery. Cars rush by on the road below, but this is one of those places that time forgot. Indeed, many of the farms here can be traced back to late Prehistoric/early Medieval times. Before that the Romans passed through with a fort at Pen Llystyn (C1st AD) and nearby, a C6th AD inscribed stone to Icorix, son of

Potentinus. The highpoint, at 210m (640ft) is just below the mast, the Arfon Transmitter. Erected in 1963 to give ITV to Llŷn, it now transmits digitally and, at 1041ft high, is the tallest structure in Wales.

Nasareth and Nebo. According to tradition, Nebo was named by the Celebrated Reverend John Jones when he preached here around 1840. Nebo is the chain of mountains from which, on one of it's peaks, Pisgah, Moses was allowed a glimpse of the Promised Land. Say no more.

These are scattered settlements, occupied by quarry workers who also kept livestock in smallholdings, and thus were able to keep body (just) and soul together. After the Second World War, the quarries closed and people left for southern Wales, England or overseas, leaving parts of the settlements to decay until they were bought as holiday homes.

The Nasareth Post Office closed in 2008.

At Llanllyfni transfer for the return journey to Lôn Eifion. The Caernarfonshire Railway was constructed in 1862 and closed in December 1964, to be re-opened as a cycle path. To the right the path takes you into Caernarfon, to the left the tarmac'd path takes you as far as Bryncir, and it's a breeze.

Pant Glas is twice renown; Bryn Terfel was raised at Nantcyll-uchaf; and next to the cycle path is the Pant Glas Aviation and Military Museum, with it's adjoining garden centre and (largely) alfresco tearoom. (Though at the time of writing the future of the Museum is not clear.) www.pgmuseum.co.uk.

Bryncir. The cycle path ends behind the Auction Mart. (The pub in the village is closed, but a kilometre down the A487 is The Goat). Route 8 does not abandon you here, but takes you to the right, up the hill and through the (rather smelly) farm of Llecheiddior Uchaf, home to pure bred Charolais cattle, and then South on minor roads. Indeed there is a choice of routes back to

Llanystumdwy and Cricieth; the minor roads are a delight, and you've met the B4411 a few hours ago.

Cricieth

Llywelyn ap Iorwerth (*Llywelyn the Great*) lived from 1173 to 1240, a Gwynedd chieftain who effectively ruled over most of Wales. He lived a life of campaigning, alliances and intrigue in various fortifications throughout Wales. Unsurprisingly he was survived by nine children, only four of whom were by his wife Joan. After his death the castle was refurbished by King Edward Ist, and the town was granted a charter in 1284, making it a free English borough. Ten years later the castle was besieged by Madog ap Llywelyn, but the constable William Leyburn with 29 men and 41 sheltering townspeople, held out all winter. In 1404, however, the castle was destroyed in the revolt of Owain Glyndŵr, and never rebuilt. The town mouldered and pottered along through the centuries. In the early C19th it had a population of just 400. But then came the Cambrian Coast Railway and it became the unspoilt, old-fashioned resort you see today. By 1895 the population had grown to 1,400+, the same as today.

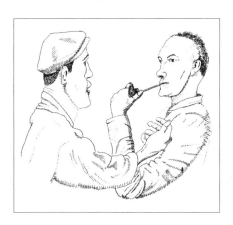

Llanystumdwy where have you been today?

160

Mynydd Graig Goch

Cricieth castle

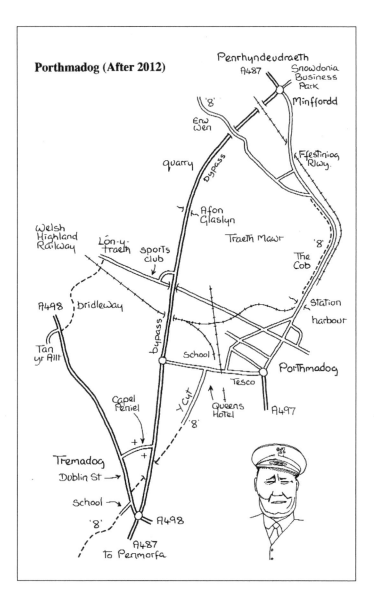

Porthmadog (After 2012)

Penrhyndeudraeth
A487
Snowdonia Business Park
Minffordd
'8'
Erw Wen
quarry
bypass
Ffestiniog Rlwy.
Afon Glaslyn
Traeth Mawr
'8'
Welsh Highland Railway
Lôn-y-traeth
sports club
The Cob
A498
bridleway
Station
harbour
Tan yr Allt
bypass
School
Porthmadog
Tesco
Capel Peniel
Y Cut
Queens Hotel
A497
'8'
+
+
Tremadog
Dublin St →
School →
'8'
A498
A487
To Penmorfa

Porthmadog

Porthmadog ("Port", as it is known) and Penrhyndeudraeth ("Penrhyn" or "Penrhyn D") have deliberately been excluded from the National Park. They command the eastern entrance to Llŷn like the Colossus of Rhodes. I've included here a couple of runs from Porthmadog, but rides to the north, south and east will have to wait for the companion volume.

In truth, cycling around Porthmadog is generally not great. It's quite hilly and there are too many main roads, but the through traffic has eased considerably now with the opening of the new bypass.

Nonetheless three 'National' cycle routes meet here. Lôn Ardudwy comes up from Barmouth and drops down from the mountains to the toll road across Afon Dwyryd between Llandecwyn and Penrhyndeudraeth. The Llwybr Trawsfynydd comes from Dolgellau, around the old nuclear power plant to Llanfrothen and Penrhyn D., and Lôn Eifion charges off to the North and Caernarfon. If there were an adequate cycle path between Black Rock, beyond Morfa Bychan, and Criccieth, Sustrans Route 8 would use that, but that remains just a footpath at present.

So, allow me to introduce to you a varied, melodramatic circular run out of Porthmadog, which for convenience I've divided into three sections, all usable independently.

Borth-y-gest

Morfa Bychan

Route 20 Porthmadog to Penmorfa via Morfa Bychan

Distance 14km (8.5mls)

Grade Popular (Easy-ish)

Parking
Porthmadog. There's a town car park behind Wilco's. Porthmadog is a busy little place with queues of traffic in summer. There is a school of thought which says the bypass won't make much difference as tourism will rise, especially with the completion of the narrow gauge railways. There's parking too at Morfa Bychan on the sands, and also at Borthygest.

Caravans/Camping
Morfa Bychan

Refreshments
Pubs and cafe's galore. I have a sneaking liking for the Harbour railway station, mainly because I'm a sucker for steam, and can stock up on postcards of grubby Black Fives. Morfa Bychan has a pub and a shop, there's probably a cafe in there somewhere too, and there's certainly one in Borth y Gest, and a cafe/bar, Shenenikins, at Black Rock, Another Roadside Attraction sort of place.

The Coast
Is this the place to mention Morfa Bychan? Mass pleasure is not really my thing, but I'm glad it exists in concentrations, and this place knocks spots off Withernsea and Cleethopes. Acres of golden sand, dunes, azure-blue sea, crashing surf, and enough room for everyone. And there's not much more to say.

20 Porthmadog- Morfa Bychan

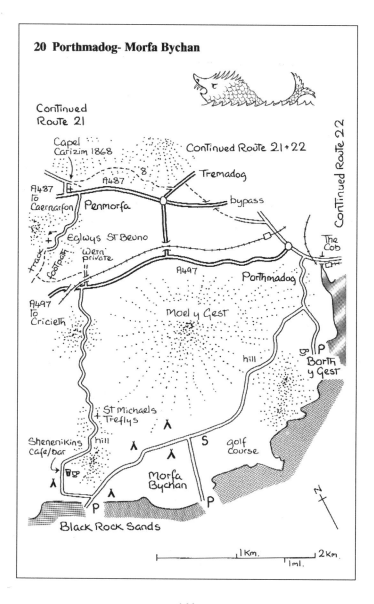

Continued
Route 21

Capel
Carizim 1868

Continued Route 21+22

A487

8

Tremadog

A487
To
Caernarfon

A487

bypass

Penmorfa

Continued Route 22

+ Eglwys St Beuno

Wern
private

The
Cob

A497

Porthmadog

Track
Footpath

A497
To
Cricieth

Moel y Gest

hill

P
Borth
y Gest

St Michaels
Treflys

Shenenikins
Cafe/bar

hill

S

golf
course

Morfa
Bychan

N

P

P

Black Rock Sands

1 Km.
1 ml.
2 Km.

The Run

From Porthmadog , the road over to Morfa Bychan has two hills on it, which would normally not be a problem, but there is traffic, cars with sand shoes on the pedals, surfboards on the roof and a caravan behind. Another short, steep hill from the Shenenikins Bar takes you up to the church of St Michaels Treflys, and a view overlooking the whole shebang. Thereafter it's a nice, little road, twisting and turning and nicely wooded at the bottom, and anywhere else on Llŷn it would be deserted, but not here.

Cross over the A497. Respect the 'Wern Private Road' sign (the house 'Wern' has medieval origins, and belonged to the Wynn's in C17th. It operated until recently as an Old Person's Home. The estate still belongs to the Williams-Ellis family.) Instead follow the track up on your left. After a short while, you're walking. This is a bridleway and a nice one too, through a garden or two, but it can be boggy in places in a wet spell. After 200 metres you emerge onto a rough track, take a right, through dappled beeches and another 200 metres brings you to Eglwys St Beuno, a discreet little church with medieval stained glass, thereafter the road is metalled. The church has been adopted by the group The Friends of Friendless Churches, and boasts a life-size carved angel, but the door is usually locked.

From here it's up and down to Penmorfa. Cross over the busy A497, keeping the converted Capel Garizim on your left. Going back to Porthmadog? Take the tiny road on your right and follow the cycle route '8' signs. They cross the A497 at the bottom of the hill and continue into Porthmadog.

21 Porthmadog - Penmorfa - Prenteg

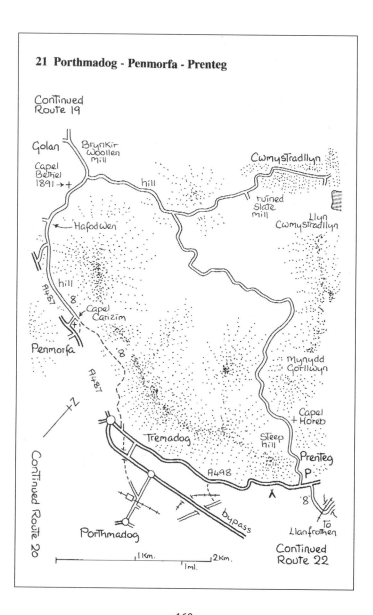

Continued Route 19

Golan

Brynkir Woollen Mill

Capel Bethel 1891 →

Cwmystradllyn

hill

ruined Slate Mill

Llyn Cwmystradllyn

← Hafodwen

hill

A487

8

Capel Carizim

Penmorfa

8

A487

N

8

Tremadog

A498

bypass

Mynydd Gorllwyn

Capel Horeb

Steep hill

Prenteg

P

To Llanfrothen

Continued Route 20

Porthmadog

1 Km. 2 Km.
1 ml.

Continued Route 22

168

Route 21 Into the Hills

Distance 19km (12mls)

Grade Popular (Medium, going clockwise. Difficult, going anti-clockwise)

Parking
Porthmadog and Prenteg. It is possible to pull off the hill road as this is unfenced.

Refreshments
None.

The Run
From Capel Garizim in Penmorfa, take the small road to the right and above the busy A487. It's a tight single track road, and the climb continues for at least a kilometre before levelling off at the Calvinistic Methodist chapel, Capel Bethel 1891. Soon after, the route takes a right turn towards Cwmystradllyn. Another kilometre of ascent and another right, towards Prenteg, and a notice which warns you of an open road ahead, with cattle grids. It is less of a warning, more an invitation.

Should you be tempted to take the cul-de-sac straight ahead, a couple of kilometres takes you to the shores of Cwmystradllyn. This reservoir was built by Llŷn Rural District Council in the early 1950's to provide drinking water for most of the peninsula, on a direct supply with no pumping required. On the hillside above is Gorseddau Quarry, a financial disaster. You can still trace the remains of the railway taking the slate to Porthmadog harbour, and the ruin is a slate mill.

The road to Prenteg is a boisterous delight, airy, free, you're

The road to Penmorfa

Llanfrothen

almost in the mountains. Half way along is a bearded lake and a kilometre of bone shaking concrete road, but this soon returns to tarmac, with a fine top dressing of sheep dung. Suddenly you're on top and the views are fantastic, down along the coast to Harlech, and a full vista of mountain, from Cadair Idris through the hills beyond Trawsfynedd and Ffestiniog to Moelwyn Bach and Mawr, Moel yr Hydd, Cnight and round to Yr Wyddfa (*Snowdon*). The reason for running this route clockwise becomes apparent as the descent is a dramatic plunge, with hairpin bends, a descent of 239m (800ft) at around 1 in 6 (17%). At the bottom my hands ached from gripping the brake levers.

It's just a kilometre or two back to Porthmadog. Opposite Tan yr Allt take a left onto a bridleway which leads you to Lôn y Traeth and back into town.

Or you can extend the run...

Route 22 Traeth Mawr

Distance 18km (11mls)

Grade Popular (Easy)

Parking
There is parking at Prenteg; near the Brondanw Arms; on the A4085 above Penrhyndeudraeth; and down on the coast near Porthmerion. And of course, Porthmadog.

Refreshments
WHR Pont Croesor; Brondanw Arms; Penrhyndeudraeth; and Porthmadog.

The Run

Take the B4410 to Llanfrothen. You share Pont Croesor over the Afon Glaslyn with the newly restored Welsh Highland Railway. You can pause here too, to view the ospreys. And a little further on is the popular Brondanw Arms, a favourite with motorised two wheeled vehicles. After the peace of the mountains the traffic comes as something of a shock, but there is only one piece of unavoidable main road, the small hill leading into Penrhyndeu-draeth. Soon after the level crossing with the Ffestiniog Railway, Sustrans route 82 is signposted onto a backstreet to the right and this takes you round the backstreets of the village, and on to a minor road to the Cob, which itself has a cycle path these days.

Porthmadog

Work began on the bypass in January 2010, and is expected to cost £34.4m, and be completed in 2012. It will provide much needed relief for a town which regularly clogs up with traffic, and will enable the two narrow gauge railways to share a terminus.

The deep water harbour was an unintended consequence of the building of the Cob 1808-1813, as the diverted river scoured out a basin. A settlement of sorts was developed by Madocks to house the navvies building the Cob. The public quay dates from 1824, being mainly used for slate, and the town grew from there. The harbour has had little commercial use since 1940, and from the 1960's it has been mainly used by pleasure craft. In 1836 the railway was completed across the Cob, the oldest narrow gauge railway in the world. At first it operated by gravity, horses travelling down in the trucks, to haul the empties back up, but in 1863 steam locomotives were introduced. A railway also came down from Croesor, serving the Park and Croesor slate quarries. In 1873, 100,000 tons of slate were exported through the harbour.

Naturally ships were built here too. There were four

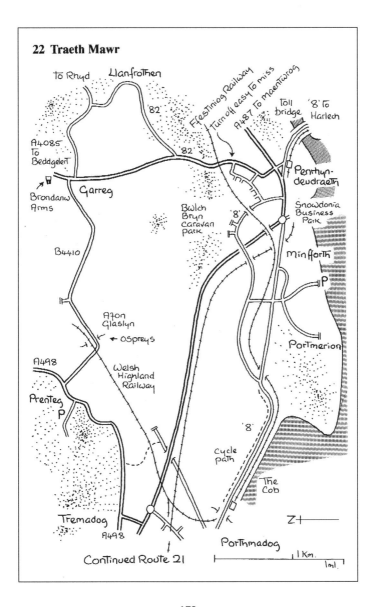

22 Traeth Mawr

To Rhyd
Llanfrothen
To Rhyd

'82'

Ffestiniog Railway
Turn off easy to miss
A487 To Maentwrog

Toll
Bridge

'8' To
Harlech

A4085
To
Beddgelert

'82'

Garreg

Brondanw
Arms

Penrhyn-deudraeth

Snowdonia
Business
Park

Bwlch
Bryn
Caravan
Park

'8'

Minfforth

P

B4410

Afon
Glaslyn

← Ospreys

Portmerion

A498

Welsh
Highland
Railway

Prenteg
P

'8'

Cycle
path

The
Cob

Tremadog

Z

A498

Porthmadog

1 Km.

1 ml.

Continued Route 21

173

shipbuilders in Borth y Gest, and over 300 vessels built in Porthmadog itself to 1914, the last few years producing fine schooners known as Western Ocean Yachts. They were designed to operate around the shallow Bae Ceredigion, as well as cross the Atlantic and the Mediterranean, and to negotiate the tricky harbours of Labrador, as well as handling heavy slate cargoes. They were described as "the ultimate development of the small wooden merchant ship in Britain". Most of them were lost in the 1914-1918 War, sunk by U-boats.

Penrhyndeudraeth

The town has grown from a fishing village, known in C19th as Cockletown. Plas yn Penrhyn was the home of Samuel Holland, and later the philosopher and activist Bertrand Russell.

Broygarth Hospital used to be the workhouse.

Minfforth Quarry opened as a sett quarry in the 1870's, and now Tarmac processes aggregates in the big crushers.

Portmeirion

Development began in 1925 as the realisation of a dream by Clough Williams-Ellis. From the start it ran as a commercial venture, the original house being converted to an hotel (Noel Coward wrote 'Blithe Spirit' here).

Porthmadog harbour

Porthmadog Cob

23 Cwm Pennant

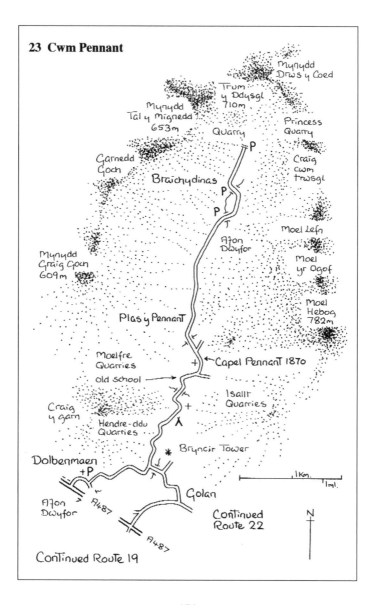

Cwm Pennant

Distance *18km (12mls)*

Grade *It's really a family run, or possibly an easy popular run*

You could throw it in as a bonus run from Route 19 too.

Parking
You can park your car at Dolbenmaen. There's a car park at the end of the valley too.

Caravans/camping
Near Llanfihangel-y-pennant is a rudimentary camp site. There are a couple of sites too on the A487. Cwm Pennant hostel is near Golan (tel 01766 530888).

Refreshments.
You're joking; the farm at Dinas sells eggs.

The Run
From the car park at Beudy'r Ddôl at the head of the valley, you are less than 10 kilometres from the summit of Yr Wyddfa (*Snowdon*), though you wouldn't know it, being virtually surrounded by rock faces and high peaks.

It's an easy run, fairly level apart from a couple of minor hills, and from Dolbenmaen it's 6 miles up the valley, and 6 miles back.

The road is narrow and unfenced in the main and, if you're lucky, you'll have it to yourselves. There are farms and some holiday places, and walkers come to park and climb, but the valley has a quiet, almost deserted feel.

Bryncir

Brynkir Tower you can see from Lodge Bridge. It was part of the Brynkir estate, broken up and sold off in 1930 following financial collapse, with the Hall left to fall into a ruin. The tower was built in 1821 by Sir Joseph Huddart to celebrate his knighthood, built as a gothic folly five storeys high. It has been restored for self-catering holidays. The stables and barn are used as an independent hostel and mountain centre (info@cwmpennan-thostel.com). The corn mill, over in Golan, was converted to wool in 1830, and still operates today (Bryncir Woollen Mill).

Slate

The remains of various slate quarries can be seen in the valley, all hopelessly optimistic and unsuccessful. At the head of the valley the Prince's Quarry, on the mountainside to the right, looked over to the Prince of Wales Quarry on the left. They opened in 1873, and closed just 13 years later. High on the shoulders of Garnedd Goch is the Cwm Ciprwth copper mine, which closed in 1894. At their height, there were 200 quarry workers in the valley. They are all disused now, leaving Cwm Pennant as 'the loveliest and most hidden of Snowdonia's valleys' in the words of local author and climber, Jim Perrin.

Cwm Pennant

Cwm Pennant church

*Experienced cyclist on
Lôn Eifion*

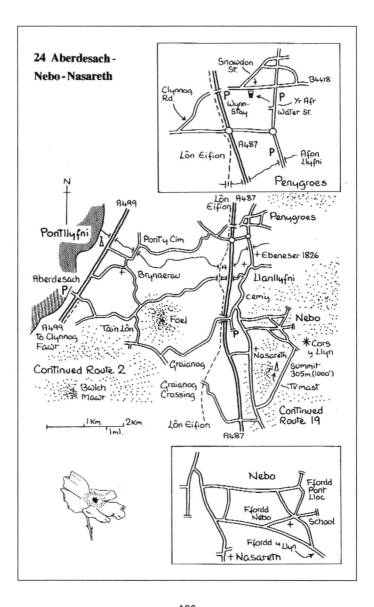

24 Aberdesach - Nebo - Nasareth

Snowdon St.

B4418

Clynnog Rd.

P

Wynn-Stay

P Yr Afr

Water St.

Lôn Eifion

A487

P

Afon Llyfni

Penygroes

N

A499

Lôn Eifion A487

Penygroes

Pontllyfni

Pont y Cim

Ebeneser 1826

Aberdesach

P

Brynaerau

Llanllyfni

Cerniy

A499
To Clynnog
Fawr

Tai'n Lôn

Foel

P

Nebo

Cors
y Llyn

Nasareth

Summit
305m.(1000')

Graianog

TV mast

Continued Route 2

Bwlch
Mawr

Graianog
Crossing

Continued
Route 19

1 Km. 2 Km.

1 ml.

Lôn Eifion

A487

Nebo

Ffordd
Pont
Lloc

Ffordd
Nebo

School

Ffordd y Llyn

Nasareth

Aberdesach to Nebo and Nasareth

Distance 22km (14mls)

Grade Popular (Medium)
Moderate in length, this run involves a climb from sea level to
305m (1000ft), none of it outrageously steep, but there is hardly
any level tarmac throughout.

Parking
Aberdesach. There is parking too in Penygroes and Llanllyfni.

Refreshments
Penygroes, Llanllyfni, and Clynnog Fawr.

This a buoyant route for those of you who want to clean out a few
cobwebs without going overboard.

Before we married, I took my intended up Great Gable, just to
make sure. My father tells me that he did the same back in 1946.
If you are a cyclist intent on matrimony, this route would be just
the job.

The Route
From Aberdesach cross the A499 and pass the burial chamber at
Pennarth. From the start the tone is set as the tiny lanes rise and
fall and curve voluptuously. Cross Afon Llyfni on Pont y Cim, a
packhorse bridge built in 1612, and take a right, climbing gently

Pont y Cim, Pontllyfni

Dyffryn Nantlle

on an old narrow lane lined with stone walls and twisted oaks. On your right you may catch a glimpse of Craig y Dinas, an Ancient British fortification.

Right again into Penygroes. In front of you is Dyffryn Nantlle (the Nantlle valley), and at the far end the huge bulk of Yr Wyddfa (*Snowdon*). At the first roundabout pick up Lôn Eifion to the right and recross Afon Llyfni, then drop down into Llanllyfni village, take a right and climb up to Nebo. This is a land of horses, old machinery, tiny warped fields and tight stone walls.

Circumnavigate the mast. On a clear day the views are terrific. Descend and turn right on the old post road through Nasareth, then work your way past the sand and gravel workings at Graianog. The direct way back is through Tai'n Lôn, a lovely wee village with a big blue shed. To extend the ride further, transfer to Route 2 (Clynnog) or even Route 3 (Around Yr Eifl).

Llanllyfni, Nebo and Nasareth: Agriculture and Slate
Traditionally the agricultural pattern here was transhumance, with animals driven onto the uplands in Spring, to the Hafod (summer dwelling), returning to the Hendre (farmhouse) for the Winter. After 1800 this whole area was turned on its head as the slate quarries opened, particularly in Dyffryn Nantlle. Hundreds were employed, thousands of tons extracted, but closures began after the war and the last large commercial quarry close in 1979. When the population increased, in Nebo and Nasareth, a crofting pattern of life emerged with the men and boys in the quarries, and the women working the croft on this rather infertile land.

Penygroes
A C19th village built around the junction of Dyffryn Nantlle and the Caernarfon-Tremadog turnpike, which opened in 1810. Social housing and industrial estates have been added to alleviate the

effects of the decline of the slate mining industry.

Antur Nantlle Cyf began in 1991 as a non-profit community business for Dyffryn Nantlle. It runs an Enterprise Centre with space for small businesses, IT training and Office facilities, and is exploring development opportunities for visitors and a possible mini-hydro electric power plant.

Llanllyfni

One of the oldest villages in Gwynedd, built around St Rhedyws' Church, itself one of the oldest in Wales, founded in C4th. The chancel was expanded in 1032 to it's present size. the main growth in the village came with the slate and metal mines in C19th.

Three chapels were built, the earliest in 1787 in Ty'n Lôn by the Baptists. The Ebeneser chapel at Felingerrig was founded in 1826 by the breakaway Baptists ('the Particular Baptists of Gwynedd' or the 'Scotch Baptists' or 'Bread and Cheese Baptists'). The Moreia chapel opened in 1871 for the Annibynnwyr, the Union of Welsh Independents or Welsh Congregational Union.

There existed in Llanllyfni a Coeden Bechod (*'tree of sin'*). The family of a deceased would bake a potato or cake and leave it to cool on the chest of the departed to absorb all their sins. This would then be placed under the Coeden Bechod and later eaten by the sin-eater. A small amount of money exchanged hands.

Cors y Llyn

Before you turn to climb up to the mast, look out over the marsh, or bog lake of Cors y Llyn, a rich habitat with St John's Wort, Cranberry, orchids and mosses, and home to the linnet and reed bunting. You may see the pupils of Ysgol Nebo and the artist Luned Rhys Parri working on a school project.

For a detailed appraisal of the landscape changes for the

whole of this part of Snowdonia, from juniper and birch scrub to birch/hazel woodland, then the succession of oak/elm, pine, alder/lime and the progressive deforestation for charcoal and grazing and grain, look up Peter Rhind and Barbara Jones The Vegetation History of Snowdonia Since the Late Glacial Period, for the Field Studies Council.

St Beuno, Pistyll

Route 25

Pilgrim's Trail Cycle Run

I have to be careful here. Did I mention that my partner, Annie, is from the USA? Massachusetts to be precise, only a spit and a prayer from the landing place in Cape Cod in 1620 of the Mayflower, so I am well aware of the creative use of the appendage 'pilgrim'. Pilgrim Pantry; Pilgrim Rum (!); Pilgrim Parking, family owned lots; Pilgrim Nuclear Power Station; Pilgrim Wrap, in case you're interested, roast turkey, avocado, tomato, jack cheese. The dictionary says a pilgrim is one who journeys to a sacred place as an act of religious devotion, AND, a person regarded as journeying to a future life. So I make no apologies for calling this the Pilgrim's Trail Run, and yes, I'm sure, if the original pilgrims had known about bicycles, they would have used them.

When your intention is to run around Llŷn, or to cycle on and to cycle off, this is what you do; Caernarfon, northern coast to Aberdaron, southern coast to Porthmadog. It's what Josie Dew did on her marathon journey around England and Wales (Josie Dew Slow Coast Home Time Warner 2003).

The pilgrims came from both sides, heading for Aberdaron, one route along the northern coast, another along the southern, except the Southern route is a matter of speculation, and on a bicycle, we must complicate it further by choosing a route which avoids the worst of the traffic. Josie Dew says 'What could have been a fine ride was ruined by stampeding convoys of vehicles and so I hurried up the underarm of the Llŷn Peninsula until I came to rest in it's armpit at Porthmadog.'

Distance

Clynnog Fawr to the End (northern coast) 44km (28mls)
The End to Porthmadog 60km (38mls)
Porthmadog to Clynnog Fawr 22km (14mls)
At it's simplest, it is a circular run of about 110km (70mls).

The Run

This is my preferred run, bearing in mind that I'm a fan of back roads, and I'm not averse to stopping these days, though you still need to maintain a rolling rhythm.

The northern coast route chooses itself:

Reference Route 2

From Clynnog Fawr, take the cycle path alongside the A499 to the roundabout junction with the B4417 near Llanaelhaearn (it's a chunky ride up to the village, and also up again towards Yr Eifl.
Reference Route 3 B4417 to Llithfaen.

Ref.	**Route 4**	and Pistyll to Nefyn.
Ref.	**Route 5**	B4417 to Tudweiliog.
Ref.	**Route 7**	From Tudweiliog take the minor roads nearest to the coast to Tŷ Hen and Methlem.
Ref.	**Route 8**	Carreg, Uwchmynydd, and on to Mynydd Mawr. Return to Aberdaron.

Coming back along the southern coast:

Reference	**Route 9**	Aberdaron, Pencaerau and up to Rhiw,
Ref.	**Route 10**	Down the steep hill to Saithbont,
Ref.	**Route 11**	Saithbont to Mynytho,
Ref.	**Route 12**	Mynytho, Rhydyclafdy, Efailnewydd, Deneio (for Pwllheli).
Ref.	**Route 17**	Deneio (Pwllheli) to Abererch. The straightforward way is to follow the

cycle path along the A497 to the B4354 junction near Chwilog.

Ref.	**Route 18**	Back road into Llanystumdwy, and back road to Cricieth. Instead, I would be sorely tempted to wander off from Abererch to Llanarmon
Ref.	**Route 17**	and Llangybi,
Ref	**Route 18**	and on to Ynys and Rhoslan.

Then both ways meet on the B4411 north of Cricieth

Ref.	**Route 19**	and follow Sustrans '8' past the 'clay sculpture' to Golan.
Ref.	**Route 21**	and on down into Porthmadog.

To complete the round,

Reference Route 19 From Golan follow the old post road and '8' to Nasareth.

Ref.	**Route 1**	From Nasareth access the minor road at Graianog, and back to Clynnog Fawr,
Ref.	**Route 2**	via Capel Uchaf. Or, to make better use of Lôn Eifion you will need to join the A487 at
Ref.	**Route 1**	at Dolbenmaen, pass the Goat to Bryncir and pick up the path there. Or, join the A487 at Dafarn Faig (note there is no access to Lôn Eifion here) and cycle up to Pant Glas,
Ref.	**Route 2**	then to Bwlchderwin and back to Clynnog Fawr.

This sounds far more complicated than it actually is.

In a way, the run as laid out above incorporates the second meaning of 'pilgrim', as every turn of your wheel leads you towards a future life, as I explained in the Introduction.

We can also define the Pilgrim run as the original pilgrims did, in terms of the sacred places en route, and these are;

(Whoa! Of course I am assuming here that churches are more sacred than chapels. I am fairly sure that Nonconformists, and I was raised as one, regard the chapel as a meeting place, rather than a sacred place in itself. Deep water for a humble cyclist. Maybe I should have called the route the Bicep to Armpit run, after all?)

Clynnog Fawr	Church of St Beuno (founded about 630)
	Ffynnon Beuno (St Beuno's well)
Llanaelhaearn	Church of St Aelhaearn (founded C7th)
	present church restored 1892
Pistyll	Church of St Beuno
Nefyn	St Mary's Church (mid C6th)
	now a maritime museum (closed)
	Ffynnon Fair (well of St Mary)
Edern	St Edern
	rebuilt 1867-1868
Tudweiliog	St Cwyfan (C7th)
	rebuilt by the Victorians.
Penllech	St Mary (on medieval foundations)
Llangwnnadl	St Gwynhoedl
Bodferin	Remains of
Aberdaron	St Hywyn and St Lleuddad
Llanfaelrhys	St Maelrhys
	plus a well
Porth Neigwl	The Saints Well
(Llanengan	St Engan)
(Llangian	St Cian)
(Llanbedrog	St Pedrog)
Pwllheli	St Peter
Abererch	St Cawrdaf
Llangybi	Ffynnon Gybi

| Cricieth | St Catharine |
| Penmorfa | St Beuno |

Pilgrimages

From the comfort of the south of England, Llŷn looked an awful long way away. Not only were there fiercesome mountains and ferocious weather in the way, but also swamps and forests, wolves, snakes and strange, foreign, incomprehensible people. To cap it all, there was the crossing of Swnt Enlli (*Bardsey Sound*), with its rip tides and boiling water, in an open boat with an oarsman or sail. As the peril (in Welsh perygl) grew, so did the sanctity and purity of the destination.

Who were they, these pilgrims (in Welsh *pererin*)? It is believed that their motives were wide and various. Like going to see The Sound of Music 67 times, some came for the pure joy. Some came for a change ("Ey up luv, Ahm fed up wi't dominoes, fance a trip t't Bardsey?"). Some were devout, some came to absolve sin, some sought answers, some to give thanks, some for a cure. It is believed that murderers and miscreants were sent to do penance and to get them out of the way (are you reading this Kenneth Clarke?).

The well-to-do travelled on horseback, but most walked, and for safety they came in groups. On arrival they would kneel in devotion, wear sackcloth, lie on ashes, eat and drink the bare minimum, and when the time came to return home, they would take with them a relic, a ring or a brooch or a cross which had been in contact with the grave of a saint. From the C11th to the C15th pilgrimage was an established part of the Christian church.

I imagine too that there was a good deal of business in this, and the 'contributions' the pilgrims made, for devotions, accomodation, guides and relics, were gratefully received. On Llŷn there were no roads at this time, travel was on tracks and paths.

There must have been times when Aberdaron was chock-a-block full of pilgrims waiting for the weather to relent so they could cross. Cwrt near Port Meudwy was excused from paying tithes by providing accomodation to those waiting to cross, and in Aberdaron Y Gegin Fawr provided sustenance. There were smaller chapels too on Anelog; Odo's chapel; Cwmdyli chapel; Cadell's church; and a chapel near Ffynnon Fair.

The saints themselves had arrived earlier, from C5th to C7th (Read *Voyages of the Celtic Saints* by Graham Panes Gwasg Carreg Gwalch 2007 for details of their European wanderings). 'Llan' meant a plot of land. Having obtained permission, the saint would build a simple church or cell, a place in which they could pray and worship. Their presence attracted others, and these men were not celibate, so there grew up a 'clas' or family community.

What do we know of the ones on this run?

St Beuno, born circa 545, was a descendant of the Prince of Powys, and founded Clynnog Fawr monastery in 616. He had a nice line in restoring to life people with severed heads, especially young maidens.

St Aelhaearn was a disciple of St Beuno.

St Edern was the son of Nudd, and an early love of Guinevere, and, although he was born here, he became Big in Brittany.

St Cwyfan, is C7th, but a mystery man.

St Gwynhoedl, a C6th missionary, and together with St Merin (born about 550, and founder of the ruined church at Bodferin) was a son of the Welsh chieftain Seithenyn. St Gwynhoedl was one of the Brothers of the College of Dunawd at Bangor Iscoed (Bangor on Dee), and a high ranking saint.

St Cadfan, 530 to590, 'the Warrior Saint', was a nobleman and a priest. He established a base at Tywyn before becoming Abbot of the monastery on Ynys Enlli, at the bidding of St Einion (born 492), the 'King' of Llŷn. Cadfan was the cousin of St Tudwal.

St Hywyn lived in Aberdaron; St Lleuddad succeeded Cadfan as Abbot of Ynys Enlli, and St Melrhys was cousin to both Hywyn and Cadfan, and travelled with them from Brittany.

St Cian, a C6th Welshman, a servant of St Peris, of Llanberis.

St Peter, the patron saint of fishermen.

St Cawrdaf was a Prince, the son of Caradog Freichfras, Prince of Brecon in C6th.

St Catherine. Because her symbol is the wheel upon which she was killed (a Catherine Wheel), her dedication may be for a church on the site of the pagan Celtic chief God, Belenos, whose symbol is also a wheel.

St Michael (the dragon-slayer). He was the archangel who defeated the devil. Churches on pagan sites, and especially sites on hills, were often dedicated to St Michael as he was best placed to stamp out the old pagan Gods.

St Cybi, 530 to 590, came from Royal stock, his mother was Gwen, sister of Non, mother of St David.

St Petrog, died 564, was the son of King Glywys of Glamorgan and Gwent. He trained in Ireland before returning to Wales, but then wanderlust took over.